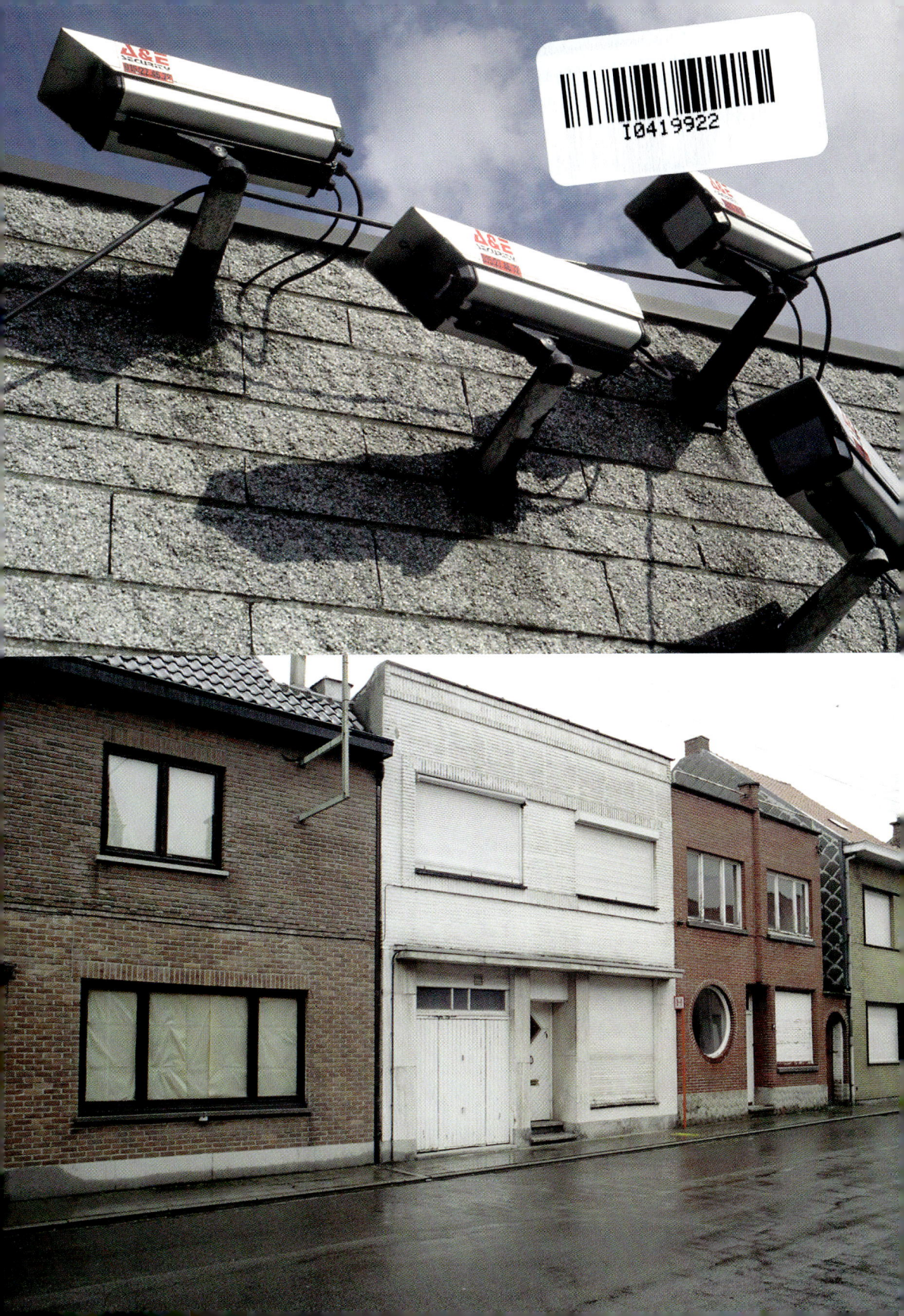

LIEVEN GEVAERT SERIES - VOLUME 1

SERIES EDITORS:

JAN BAETENS

HILDE VAN GELDER

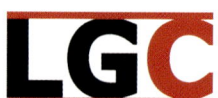

LIEVEN GEVAERT RESEARCH CENTRE FOR PHOTOGRAPHY AND VISUAL STUDIES

WWW.LIEVENGEVAERTCENTRE.BE

Els Vanden Meersch

Paranoid obstructions

Essay
Hilde Van Gelder

Poem
Alice Evermore

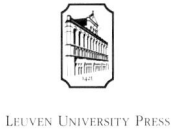

LEUVEN UNIVERSITY PRESS

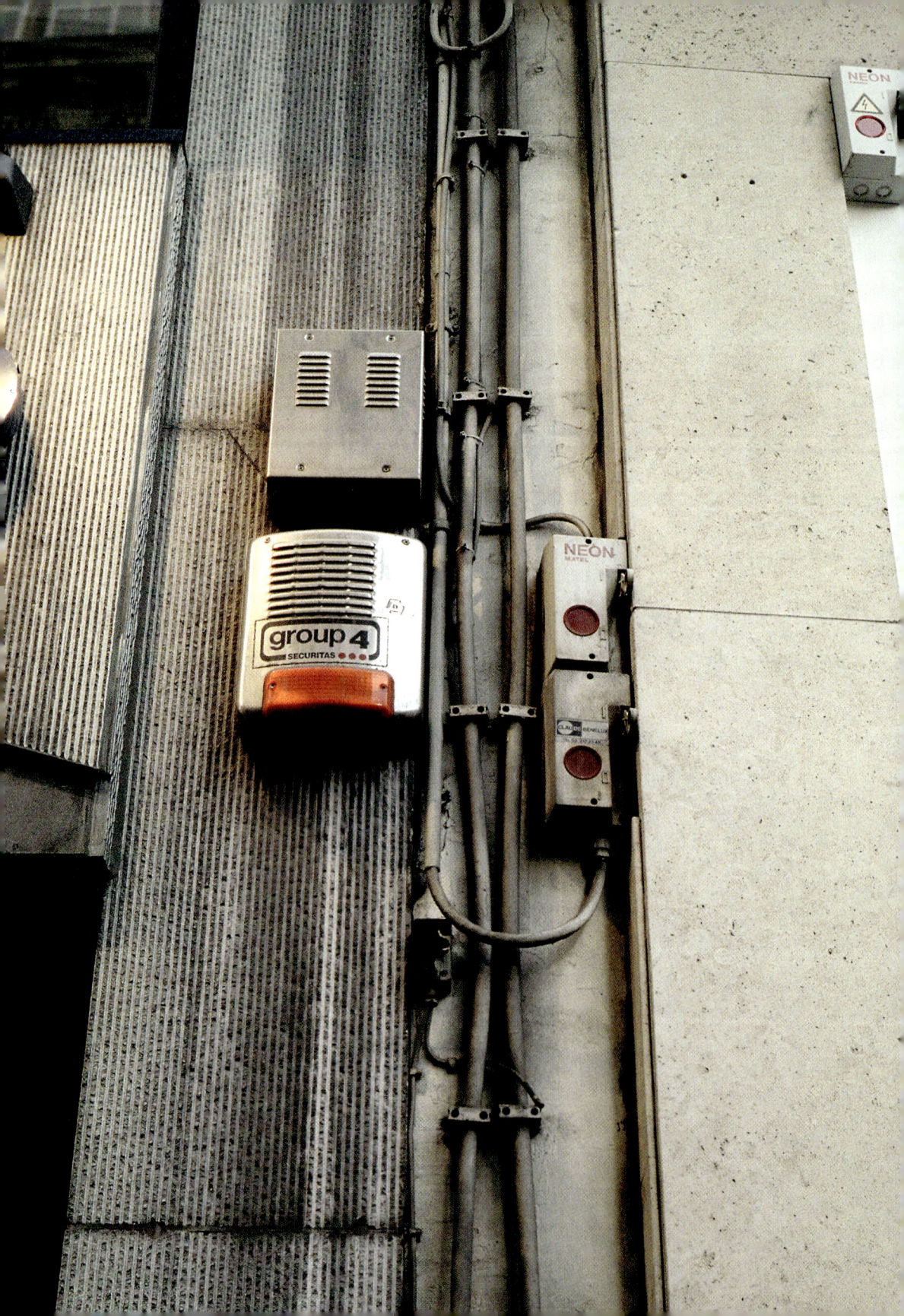

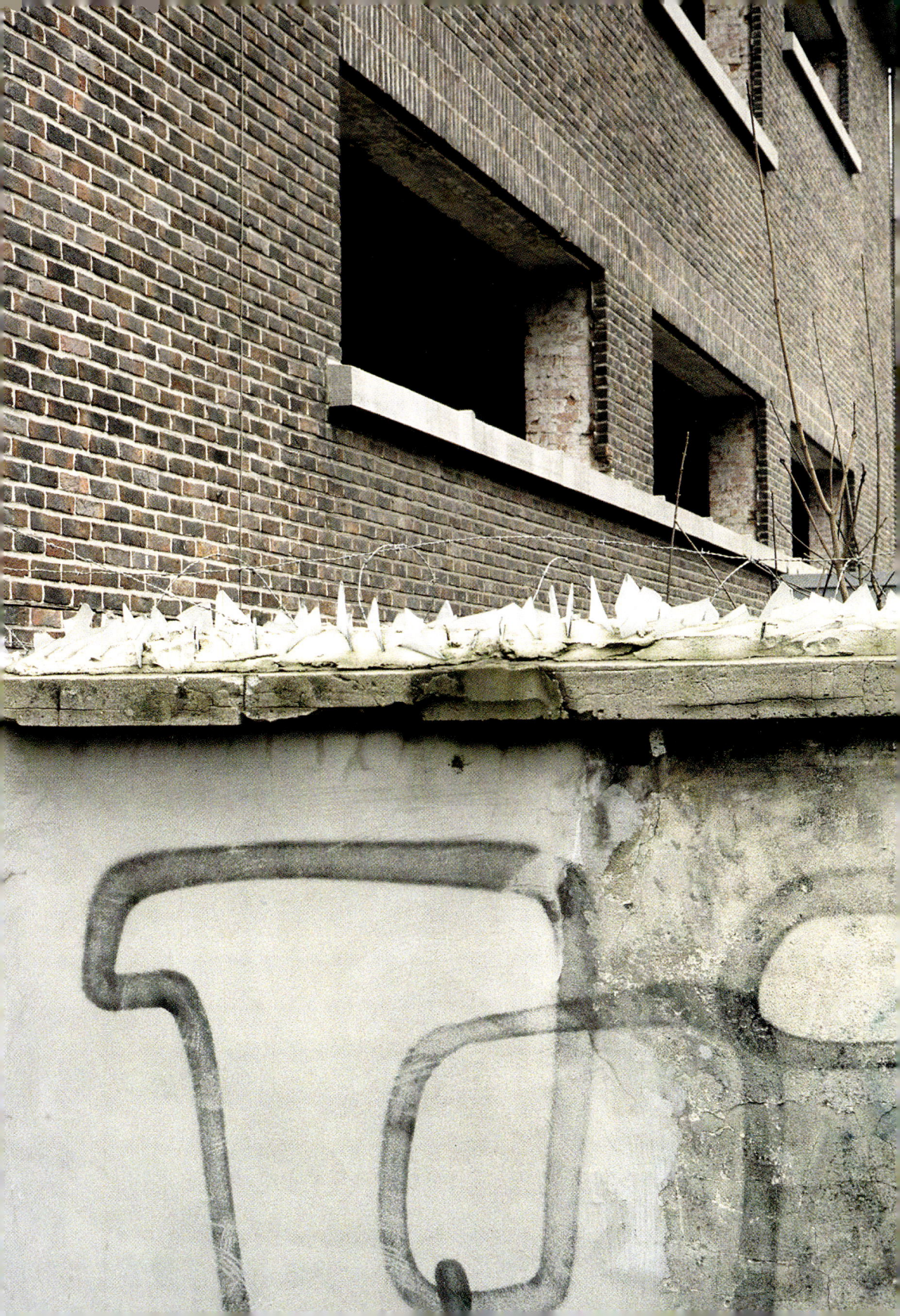

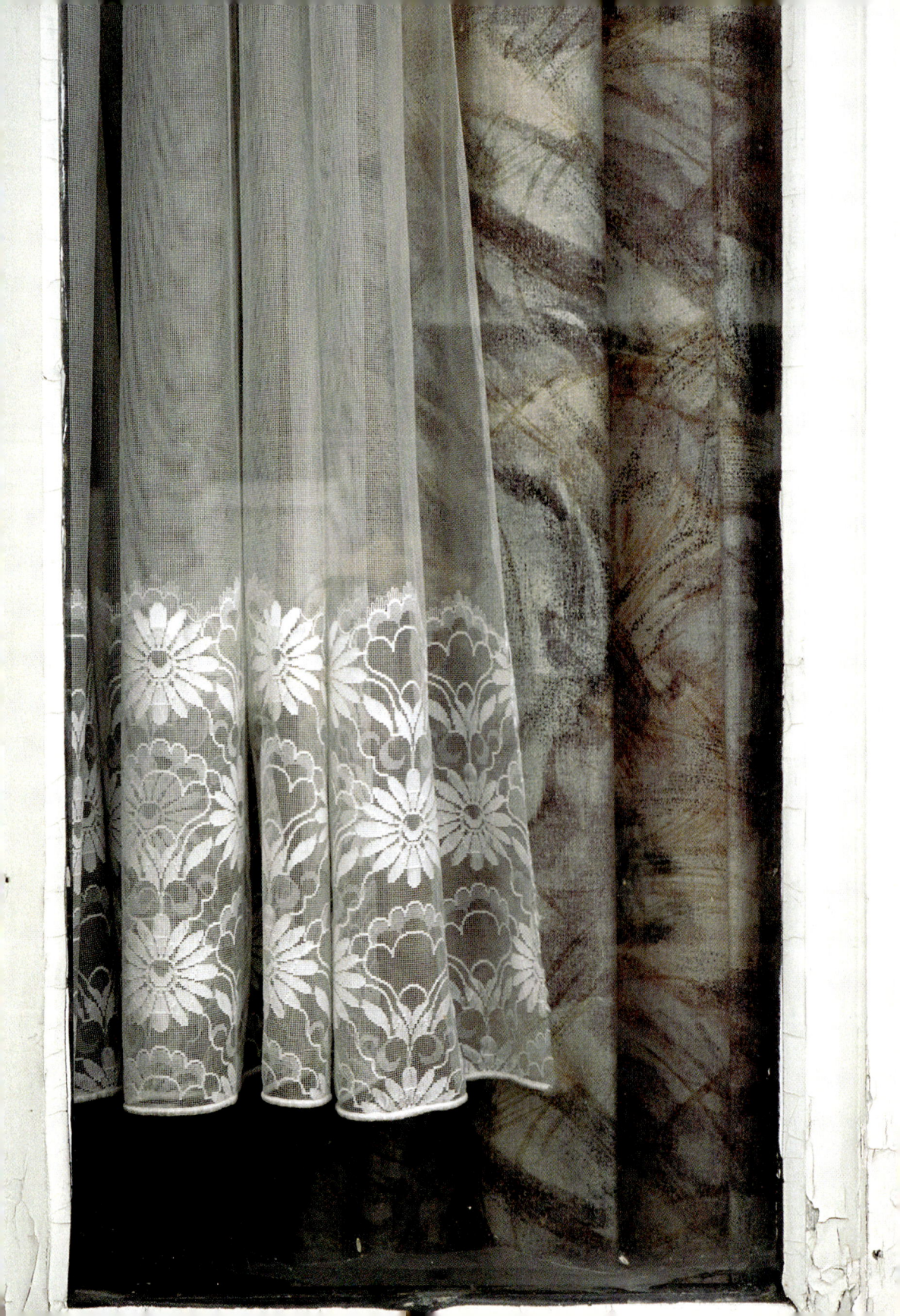

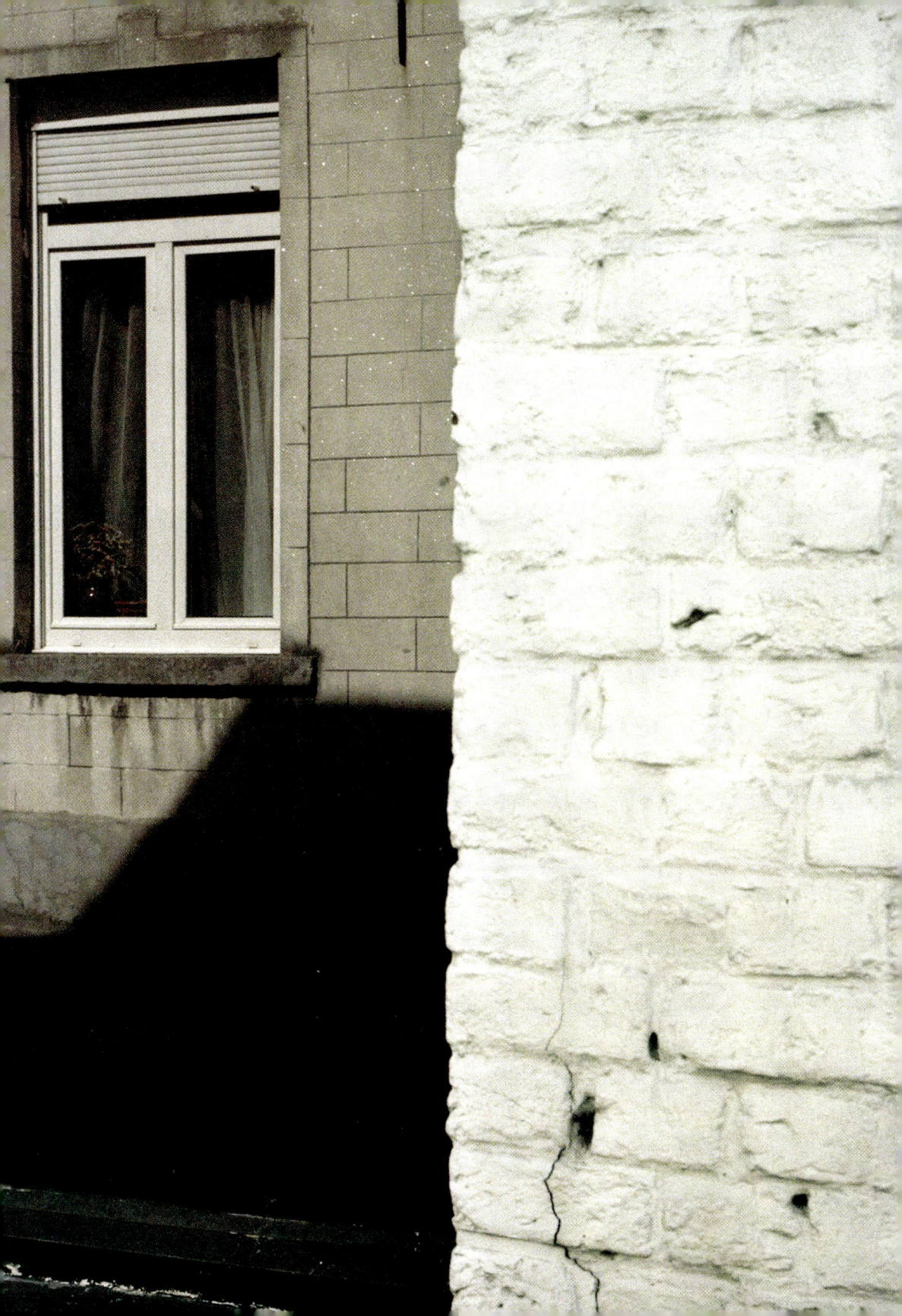

War is coming home

Hilde Van Gelder

'Eye walls:' – faciality

The substantial photographic archive that Els Vanden Meersch has collected since 1996, is ordered in a classification system of 25 sections.[1] The most eye-catching note in that index is probably the sixth: 'Eye Walls:'. This is, indeed, a neologism. Yet any observant person can conjure up, even without any accompanying visual material, an image in his mind. The term points to walls with eyes. It indicates walls that can 'look'. The idea that walls might be able to stare at us, is hardly new. The most famous example is probably that of the ultramodern villa Arpel in Jacques Tati's film *Mon Oncle* (1958). This futuristic house, with its facade incorporating two round porthole-like windows, looks like a post-surrealist house come to life straight out of one of René Magritte's paintings. Completely surrounded by a wall, this house, including a monstrous garage with a massive two-eyed opening and closing gate, is a fortress, a petrified apparatus for spying on the unsafe outside world.

André Malraux, too, strengthened by historic examples, already knew that walls possess a strange ability to see. In the last, revised edition of his *Le musée imaginaire* (1965), he inserts an important passage in the third chapter in which he represents a *Tower with Faces* from Khmer art (12th-13th century) next to a Malinese fetishist cave.[2] The striking factor in these mirroring pages, which allow themselves to be visually analysed as an elementary Rorschach test, is that the figurative carved face in Angkor Thom has half-open eyes and a full mouth with thick lips, whereas the African Dogon artefact is just a geometric-abstract rendering of two adjacent, quasi-square holes. Underneath there is an oblong mouth opening, although that is practically entirely blocked by gigantic tree stumps and boulders – so it can be reduced to a thin horizontal slit. The figurative face of the Cambodian artefact didn't leave us in any doubt as it was, but even without that accompanying 'mirror image' it was perfectly clear: we view the entrance to that cave as if it were a face. It stares at us, and we look back, fascinated.[3]

It doesn't seem obvious for people to be able to see a surface with a number of holes as a face. Yet it is part of the fundamental principles of human vision, which have meanwhile been well charted by visual semiotics. In *Languages of Art* (1968), for instance, Nelson Goodman convincingly argues that the relationship of similarity between a representation and the reality to which it refers is always based on symbolic relations, not natural or innate ones.[4] People share a conventionally determined set of visual concepts, which among others enables them to *see* certain compositions of lines and / or colours as a face.

Gilles Deleuze and Félix Guattari devote an important chapter in their key work *A Thousand Plateaus* (1980) to this special human skill. Under the title 'Year Zero : Faciality' they describe the face as resulting from, emerging from a structured system of relations between a white wall and a black hole.[5] The face, for them, is a flat visual surface that begins to leave a faint imprint *on* the white wall and *in* the black hole. But these relations are changeable and unstable: for Deleuze and Guattari it might as well be a black wall and a white hole allowing a face to take shape. This concerns a continuous mechanism of movement, generating 'facial' meaning. Approaching the photo series *Paranoid obstructions* from this angle, we can virtually see an endless sequence of 'faces', of emerging looks from 'eye walls' wanting to communicate with us.

The face as a bunker

The face is "a horror story", according to Deleuze and Guattari, because it unsettles us. It results from "an abstract machine of faciality (visagéité)".[6] These abstract machines of faciality randomly use any visual element. And so body cavities other than eyes are capable of generating facial meaning. In certain circumstances, for instance, we can have the feeling that a wide-open mouth is 'gaping' at us. But also non-human creatures can stare. Those, too, are objects with a peculiar kind of corporality, leading their own lives in the reality that we share with them. They communicate with us through the surface that is their 'face', exactly as in the case of communication between living beings. Tati shows this very didactically, when he repeatedly makes Mr and Mrs Arpel appear at night, each in front of one single lighted upstairs window of their villa. As such, they become, as it were, the paranoid, lively pupils of the eye wall that is the facade of their house.

This process of 'facialization' from an abstract field of facial elements does not emerge from an immediate likeness between the image and the reality to which it refers.[7] In fact, Deleuze and Guattari conclude, we can view any surface with a specific semiotically recognizable visual structure *as* a face, the reason being that each face, as an object of perception, always has a disembodied quality. Indeed, the face only allows itself to be known when it has visually detached itself from the 'body' to which it belongs. The face only exists in the act of perceiving, as a disembodied 'sur-face'. Obviously, this doesn't mean that this 'body' really has to be absent or has to disappear, but that the face that we meet, *in* its facial experience, is no longer immediately coded by the body. It has been abstracted from it, as it were. It has detached itself, and only left a 'vague physical' trace. This entails that detecting a face has something dehumanized, from the beginning, and hence also something inhuman. "Bunker-face," they write strikingly.[8]

It is those abstract machines of faciality that are responsible for the decoding, the loosening of facial data relating to the body. But at the same time, it is also those that allow a recodification or even surcodification of the face resulting from the facial genesis. In the confrontation from look to look, from face to face, new possibilities of meaning emerge. Deleuze and Guattari name the signifier that starts up the abstract machines of faciality as the face of Christ himself: "*facies totius universi*. Jesus Christ superstar".[9] The Machine of faciality that we take as a frame of reference in the Western visual language, begins in the year zero, at the birth of Christ. It is He, they argue, who sets into motion all facialization processes, by spreading his own image, as if he were a central computer, an all-seeing third eye, capable of moving across a wall or a white screen that serves as a general surface of reference.

The representation of the unrepresentable / unimaginable

From the moment at which the face of Christ becomes the point of reference in the Western visual language, the prototypical history of the white Man develops, with the well-known face: a white skin with dark eye sockets (white wall / black hole). The first deviations from this, which we already see in Medieval and Renaissance art, immediately take on racist or pejorative connotations: yellow man, black man, second- and third-category men, dark surfaces with lightened holes (black wall / white hole). From the racist point of view, Deleuze and Guattari claim, there is no 'exterior', there are no people 'on the outside' [*dehors*]. There are only people who should be like we are, and whose crime it is that they are not.[10]

W.J.T. Mitchell, in his book *What do pictures want*, which is to be published shortly, makes a comparison between the pose of the by now world famous Iraqi war photos of 'the man in the monk's hood' – roaming the internet as a ghost named 'the hooded man / l'homme à la cagoule' – and the pose of a stumbling, supported Christ as 'the man of sorrow' as we can see it in several Renaissance representations (a.o. by Andrea Mantegna).[11] The confusion we feel upon watching the images of 'the hooded man' is linked with the renewed interpretation they offer of the idea of a *facies totius universi*: Christ's passion experienced by an Arab, belonging to a different religion, by someone who should be 'outside' – with all possible implications linked to that. Such war images, with their clear evocation of Christian martyrdom, go around the world in newspapers and on television. At breakfast or over dinner, they show us the unimaginable, but in the blink of an eye they have gone again: the page is turned quickly, the TV image gone irrevocably. But as afterimages, they linger in the collective memory all the more powerfully.

The unimaginable happens. We, passive observers of that horror, haven't been blinded, but stare, struck dumb, unable to say the unspeakable. Looking at photos of terror, like recently of the hostages in Beslan, we are lost for words. On 23 October 2004, Mitchell introduced to the audience, in the context of the word-image conference in the Antwerp Film Museum, a semiotic scheme on which this analysis is based.[12] It can be described as follows: Mitchell divides a circle horizontally into two halves. In the upper half, he puts a small circle, with a double horizontal line inside, and underneath another small circle. This is a semiotic representation of a blindfolded face screaming (zone of the unimaginable). In the lower half, we see exactly the opposite: a circle with two small circles inside, like staring little eyes, with two horizontal lines at the level of the mouth: this figure has been gagged (zone of the unspeakable). Both zones relate to each other like an inevitable vicious circle.

The exceptional power of the series *Paranoid obstructions* lies in the fact that it represents what cannot be shown, yet without showing it. It thus allows for a representation of the unimaginable.[13] The entire series refers implicitly to what it cannot represent as such (unrepresentable, for unimaginable): images of war and terrorism in a country far away, but that are, in their absent horror, all the closer to home. The images use a visual abstraction mechanism that allows metaphorical distance with respect to the themes in question, and reflection. At the same time, they make the unspeakable sayable. We are no longer passive, dumbfounded receivers of horrible signals. The martyrs have ascended into heaven, the 'man of sorrow' has risen and gone. What returns is his abstract face in the form of a vague bodily trace. *Paranoid obstructions*, saccadic perceptions, fleeting looks, in the blink of an eye, momentary flashes following one another in an endless series, yet never succeeding in really seeing what they are looking at. The spaces look, but don't see. They are blind, the words cut off, like a blindfolded victim of terror at the moment of decapitation. A final, blinded scream into emptiness, then the irrevocable end.

The portrait, today

Els Vanden Meersch calls her installations and photos portraits. The notion of the portrait is a historically laden term, referring to a genre that is very important in the visual artistic tradition. Traditionally, it is a figurative genre that, following the imitation theory, dominant in Western art for several centuries, based itself on the principles of a realistic relation of similarity or likeness between the representation and the represented. The fundamental condition of the portrait genre is, in this respect, that the image enables the observer to recognize the individual that is represented. Bart Verschaffel, in an important text, defines the classical portrait as follows: "it represents a real individual. To call a representation 'a portrait', or to approach it as a portrait, means that one relates to something that *exists, or has existed in reality*. The portrait confirms that someone *has really existed*."[14] This is a definition that applies to the figurative genre, but that can be used, by extension, to call abstract images of faciality portraits.

For, because of that emergence of a tangible feeling of existence, the portrait genre is a particularly physical genre. In the Western visual tradition, the portrait is an incarnated image. Following the *mandylion*, or the cloth on which Christ had his true, divine face imprinted forever, the portrait carries the traces of a body.[15] Thus, the portrait also re-embodies the person in question. But the representation in the portrait does not allow us to know it *as a body*. It is only an abstract machine of faciality, allowing facial genesis. The portrait, even the most realistic-mimetic one, needs to be discovered by us as a 'sur-face', as a disincarnated or disembodied face that presents, tangibly yet abstractly, no more than the traces of the body to which it belongs. This confrontation happens in the blink of an eye; it is the shock experience of an unintended look, saccadic but all the more paranoid.

The '(sur-)face' that momentarily emerges from the abstract field of faciality, does not necessarily look with two eyes / holes. It may be composed of a multiplicity of peepholes, or – analogous to the all-seeing third eye of Christ himself – of just one single viewing objective. Deleuze and Guattari, too, name the liminal figures of the face as consisting of two basic categories – analogous to the portrait tradition in painting: the frontal type and the profile. A frontal image necessarily offers a multiplicity of eye sockets and perspectives. But profiles confront the observer with only one eye. The image becomes cyclopean, as it were, synthetic, omnipotent yet also less balanced.

The visual metaphor of a disembodied look that still carries with it the traces of its corporeality, is omnipresent in Els Vanden Meersch' photos. We never find a human body in her images, yet these works radiate corporeal presence. So, an abstract face can prove as well that someone has existed. The body has then, in the faciality of its look, become the prosthesis of itself. It stares, from behind a twitching net curtain, or via the literal optical extension of a surveillance camera or rear-view mirror. The body is never represented in a realistic-mimetic way, yet is constantly present. By renaming the images as portraits, Vanden Meersch also clearly places them – very coherently – in that tradition of representation of the incarnated image that only allows itself to be known in the momentary meeting with a disembodied face.

In fact these images widen the horizon of expectation of the portrait genre in general, but that is a merely formal element. More interestingly, they broaden and enrich the possibilities of meaning of the portrait genre. In the present era of the culture of visual experience, in which the 'man of sorrow' freely roams the internet, in an entirely extra-artistic context, it is impossible – for utterly tautological – to directly handle, within the artistic tradition of representation, those traditional-iconographic data. But present-day art can evoke him indirectly, though, generating a fundamental process of reflection around the artistic representation of the unrepresentable / unimaginable.

Gasping for breath / 'vents:'

Tati's *Mon oncle* draws the portrait of a dazzling yet daunting nuclear family of the future. The heavily glazed architecture surrounding them, in which they breathe, actually appears to stifle them in the most paranoid moments in the film. Thus the couple Arpel gets locked into the garage at a certain moment, when their dog, a keeshond, accidentally minces past the electronic eye and the gate is shut with a frightful bang in their faces. Their helpless heads, appearing in front of the two 'eye holes' of the gate, seem to be gasping for breath. They act like headless chickens.

The photo series *Paranoid obstructions* does not show 'amputated' heads. Nevertheless, the look of these images generates an oppressive feeling of a lack of breath, in the metaphorical sense. You don't just read the graffito slogan, accidentally found by the artist: "I can't breath [sic] I became a glass". What this image shows, literally, can also be seen, repressed, in the other images in the series. They tell a story of a continuous cat-and-mouse game between 'disembodied faces', of a continuous spying and being spied on. Without ever getting to see anyone, you constantly feel vicious or stealthy looks, you imagine the bricked-up walls as gagged mouths that want to scream and whose breath is being taken away.

In Els Vanden Meersch' photos those quickly effaced, traumatic representations have been coded, and recoded at the same time. By evoking places where the trauma could take place, without us having to see or experience it again, a reflexive process evolves. This disembodied confrontation with the abstract face of the unrepresentable / unimaginable allows for ways of dealing with the trauma. We can think about it, and linger over these images longer than the blink of an eye. They don't force us – unlike the all too confrontational physicality of direct images of terror – to zap away quickly. By taking a step back, this photographic series creates a new closeness, allowing grief and contemplation.

The roving, third eye – 'Spies: (spyholes in doors)'

But this renewed form of involvement or closeness to current events in the world is hardly noncommittal. Els Vanden Meersch purposefully opts to represent places that are recognizable for anyone who knows their way around the present-day Belgian urban development landscape. The places we see, are part of our everyday context. The dramas to which the abstract faces detaching themselves from eye walls, testify, only become more tangible. They could happen here. War is coming home.[16] The opening page of the collage series *Paranoid obstructions* almost literally shows Mitchell's scheme: a vertical setting, the semiotic representation of the unspeakable at the top – us, passive-Western onlookers: the eyes frontal and wide open, but the mouth gagged. Just below, there is the figure of the unthinkable or the unimaginable, its eyes – in several horizontal lines – blindfolded, with underneath a mouth bright as an acute alarm signal.[17]

In the series itself, we find, alternating, frontal looks and looks in profile. But sometimes the artist also offers us, thanks to the camera angle she chooses, an intermediate perspective, i.e. as viewers we have to deal with an imperfect profile. That is the case, for instance, in the image of a closed window, with an opened twin window next to it, as if it were winking. The one eye seems to be staring at you frontally, while the other eye is barely looking, even turning away. The result is the combination of a dominant look and a hesitant look, of a fixed and a deviating perspective at the same time. As such, the images clearly indicate they don't want to phrase any answers. They raise questions, and let meanings develop in a multiplicity of angles.

The frequent mirror motifs in *Paranoid obstructions* strengthen this idea of constantly changing angles on the same subject. The mirrors photographed generate a momentary look, but immediately shift it again. For in fact they mirror nothing special: they only offer a renewed confrontation with the same, like an endless loop or a continuous Rorschach test. Thus potential meanings develop, but they don't allow themselves to be pinned down or fixed. "The mirror", Deleuze and Guattari write, "is but secondary in relation to the white wall of faciality".[18] They mean that the mirror does not refer to a concrete individual or subject, but only to a face that emerges in the mirror image and that is only linked with the body itself via an awkward, abstract process of tracing. The iced mirror forming the final image of *Paranoid obstructions*, hits you in the face chillingly and definitively with this conclusion.

'Panoramic (distant)' looks

Some images from the series *Paranoid obstructions* seem to be interiors of prisons, or at least buildings with an oppressively forceful impact on the people who can circulate in it. We see surveillance cameras, blocked-off passages, signals or bars. Striking, too, are the many badges and signs indicating a direction of circulation. In everyday life, we experience such things as entirely matter-of-course. It is unsettling how seldom we consider the disturbing effect of derelict, bricked-up facades, or how meekly we allow ourselves to be led through the maze of a circuit of corridors. In *Mon oncle*, too, Tati has the main character, Monsieur Hulot, circulate compulsively along the road markings through and around the remarkably clean factory building of his brother-in-law, Monsieur Arpel. Apart from factories, hospitals are the prototypical example *par excellence* of a neurotically organized, clean environment. Both types of spaces are subtly given a prominent place in *Paranoid obstructions*.

In *Discipline and Punish*, Michel Foucault extensively discusses the fairly obvious way in which we deal with such oppressive spaces.[19] In reality, it is far from obvious, he stresses. No matter how much we have grown used to it, it is certainly no universal law that people should function in bunker-like, inhuman surroundings. Foucault takes the example of prison as a case study. In its present-day form, this concept is only about 150 years old, he remarks, which as such is a fairly short period. Yet this period has been enough to make prisons into something entirely banal and normal in our everyday living environment. But they are not. Precisely measured (detention)time, meticulous description of movements within the space, panoptical systems of lighting which lend the bars – separating inside from outside – a glorious brilliance: the control urge characterizing the prison model is emblematic for our present-day interaction with reality. For Foucault, prison is a metaphor, a mirror image for our way of life 'outside', a '*dehors*' which we can only imagine with the most strenuous effort.

Prison, Foucault finally states, creates a paradoxical effect. Instead of 'healing' delinquents, it just shapes them even further. The prison model confirms and strengthens the system. For a number of those who eventually get out, there is a feeling of *been there, done that*. They have already been stigmatised, and don't have much to lose. Many fall back into their old habits exactly because of the stigma, can't seem to find the strength to break free from them. That feeling of paralysis is also evoked in Els Vanden Meersch' photos, sometimes even up to the point of apathy. In the short-term facial confrontation with the abstract face of this stranger within ourselves, we recognize the terrorist or the criminal we could or might have been.

Els Vanden Meersch' photos in no way allow an analysis as political statements, nor do they constitute a direct indictment of anything whatsoever. She describes her images as poetic herself, indicating that her photo archive does not allow a reduction to mere documentation.[20] Yet the photographic images should not be read as a documentary either. They offer no further interpretation whatsoever of the situation they represent or reflect on. On the contrary, they raise questions and leave answers open. This generates a certain mental malaise. But along with the metaphorical distance between the images and the context they sketch, their involvement with the situations depicted is heightened. They never become overly pictorial or noncommittal tableaux. Their explosive level of critical-realistic potential is far too high for that.

Paranoid obstructions offers a convincing way out of the overly confrontational character of the traumatizing images it so strikingly evokes. Thanks to the avoidance of tautological repeat mechanisms and opting for the confrontation with the photographic image as an abstract machine of faciality, a momentary yet deeply influential exchange of looks is realized, in the 'physical vague' spaces – so far and yet so near – that Els Vanden Meersch has a unique feeling for.

1   The Index – made in the spring of 2004 – contains the following terms, in this order: "Spies: (spyholes in doors) – surveillance equipment – Mirrors: - Signals: - Berlin Wall: - Eye Walls: - Blocked (bricked up) – Bars: - Panoramic (distant) – Ordinary facades: - Graffiti: - Door numbers and doorbells: - Doors: - Central spaces – Light sources and physical vague spaces: - Interiors: - Windows (indefinite) – Blue-painted windows (breendonk): - Curtains: - Glass (panes) – Blinds: - Glass fragments: - Stairs: - vents: - Miscellaneous".

2   A. Malraux, *Le Musée Imaginaire,* third revised edition (Paris: Gallimard, 1965), 172-173 (fig. 115 and 116).

3   For a Lacanian approach to this problem, cf. J. Elkins, *The Object Stares Back. On the Nature of Seeing* (San Diego: Harcourt, 1998).

4   N. Goodman, *Languages of Art. An Approach to a Theory of Symbols,* [1968] 2nd revised edition (Indianapolis: Hackett Publishing Company, 1976), 6-10.

5   G. Deleuze and F. Guattari, *A Thousand Plateaus* (1980), transl. B. Massumi (Minneapolis: University of Minnesota Press, 1987), 167.

6   Ibid., 168.

7   In the French original, Deleuze and Guattari speak of "visagéification": cf. Id., *Mille Plateaux* (Paris: Minuit, 1980), 209.

8   Id., *A Thousand Plateaus*, 171.

9   Ibid., 176.

10 Ibid., 178. The quotation of the French "dehors" is in the original text on p. 218.

11 The most striking image in the series, in which the man, with something like a horrible magician's hat pulled over his head, balances on a cardboard box while holding wires in each hand that will electrocute him if he falls off, was to be seen, among others, at the exhibition *Inconvenient Evidence: Iraqi Prison Photographs from Abu Ghraib* in the International Center of Photography in New York (September-November 2004). It can be consulted at, among others, http://www.icp.org.

12 Not as yet published, but to appear in his book *What do pictures want?* (Chicago: University of Chicago Press, 2005).

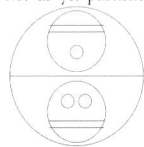

13 In Dutch, the notion of 'onvoorstelbaar' at the same time means 'unimaginable' and 'unrepresentable'.

14 B. Verschaffel, 'Kleine theorie van het portret', *De Witte Raaf*, 81 (September-October 1999): 2.

15 I have based this passage on an exceptionally enlightening text by Barbara Baert, 'De sluier en het gelaat. Het *mandylion* en het auteursportret in het licht van de vroegmiddeleeuwse beeldtheorieën', to be published in J. Papy (ed.), *Geleerdenportretten – geleerde portretten* (Leuven University Press, 2005).

16 I obviously refer to Martha Rosler's important critique on the Vietnam war, namely her collage series *Bringing the War Home* (1966-72).

17 See the image of the lit-up alarm system on p. 4 of this book.

18 Deleuze and Guattari, *op. cit.* (n. 5), 171.

19 M. Foucault, *Surveiller et punir. Naissance de la prison* (Paris: Gallimard, 1975). Especially the final part, on prison, is relevant here: pp. 267-343 – *Disciplin and Punish: the Birth of the Prison*, transl. A. Sheridan (New York: Pantheon, 1977).

20 S. Siffer, 'Een visueel geheugen als mogelijkheidszin' / 'A visual memory as sense of possibility', in Els Vanden Meersch. *Transient constructions* (Antwerp: Landschap&Portret vzw and Genk: FLAC©, 2003), n.p.

Hilde Van Gelder wishes to thank Jan Baetens, Willem Hesling, W.J.T. Mitchell, Pieter Van Reybrouck, Els Vanden Meersch and Stefan Siffer.

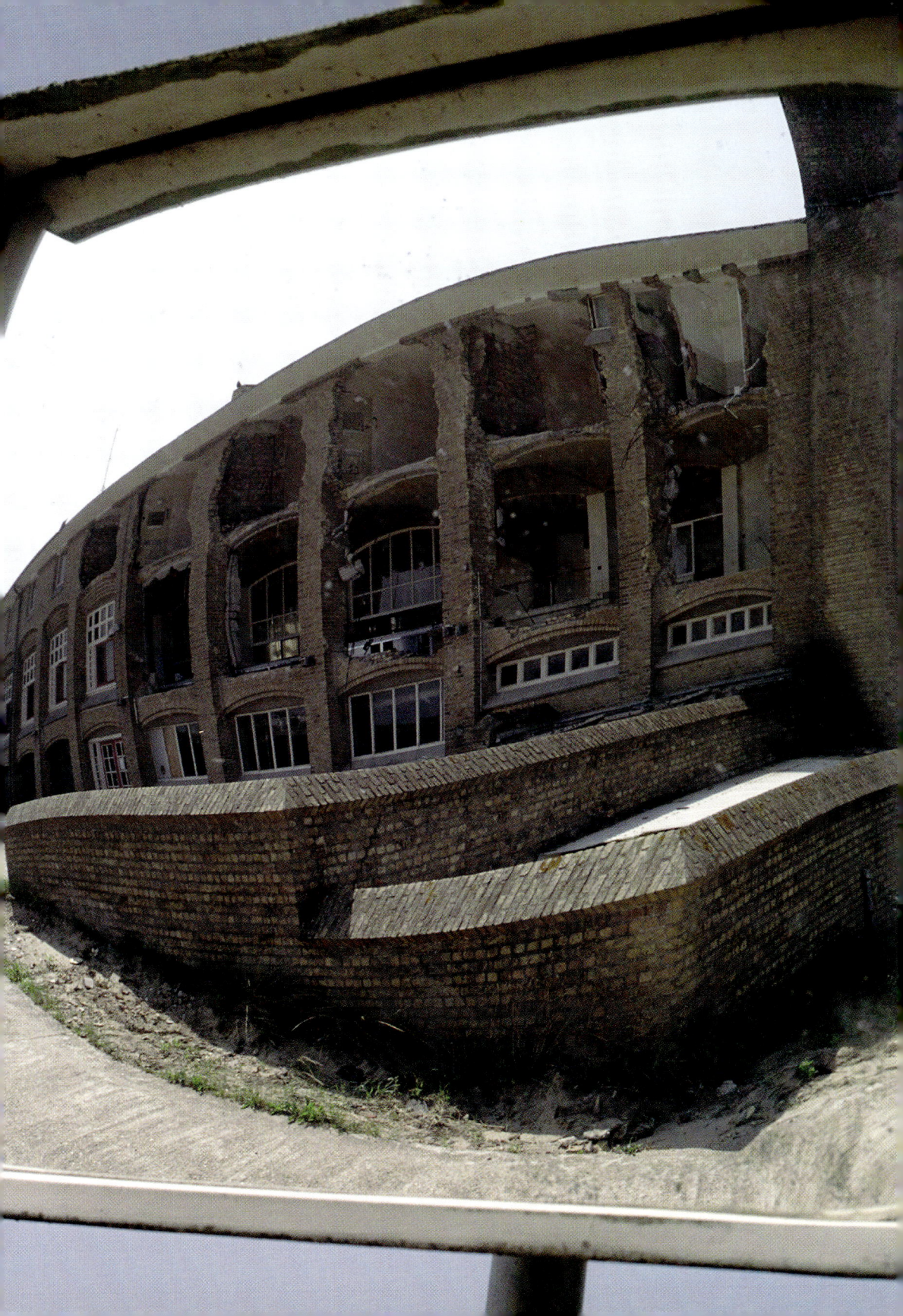

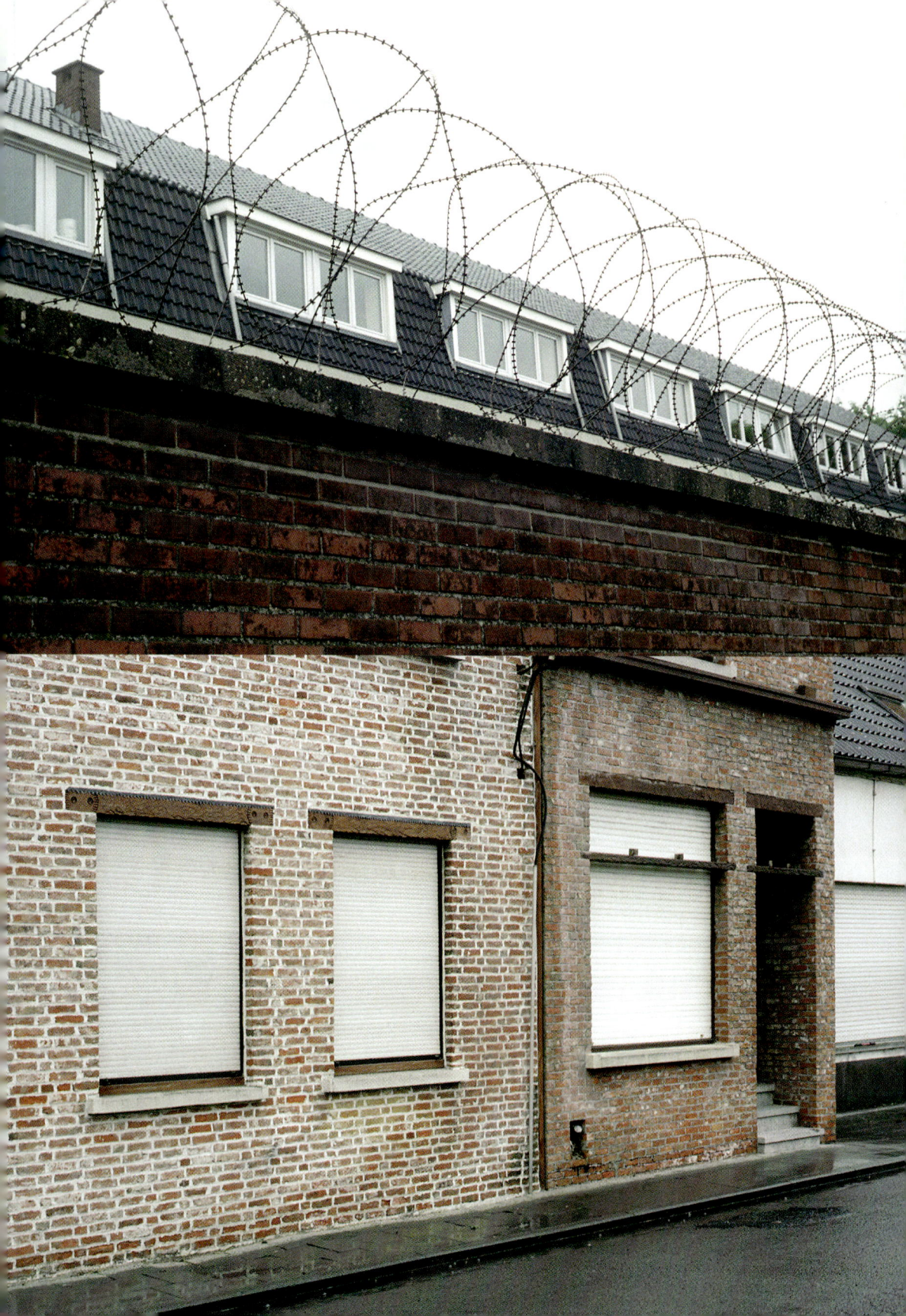

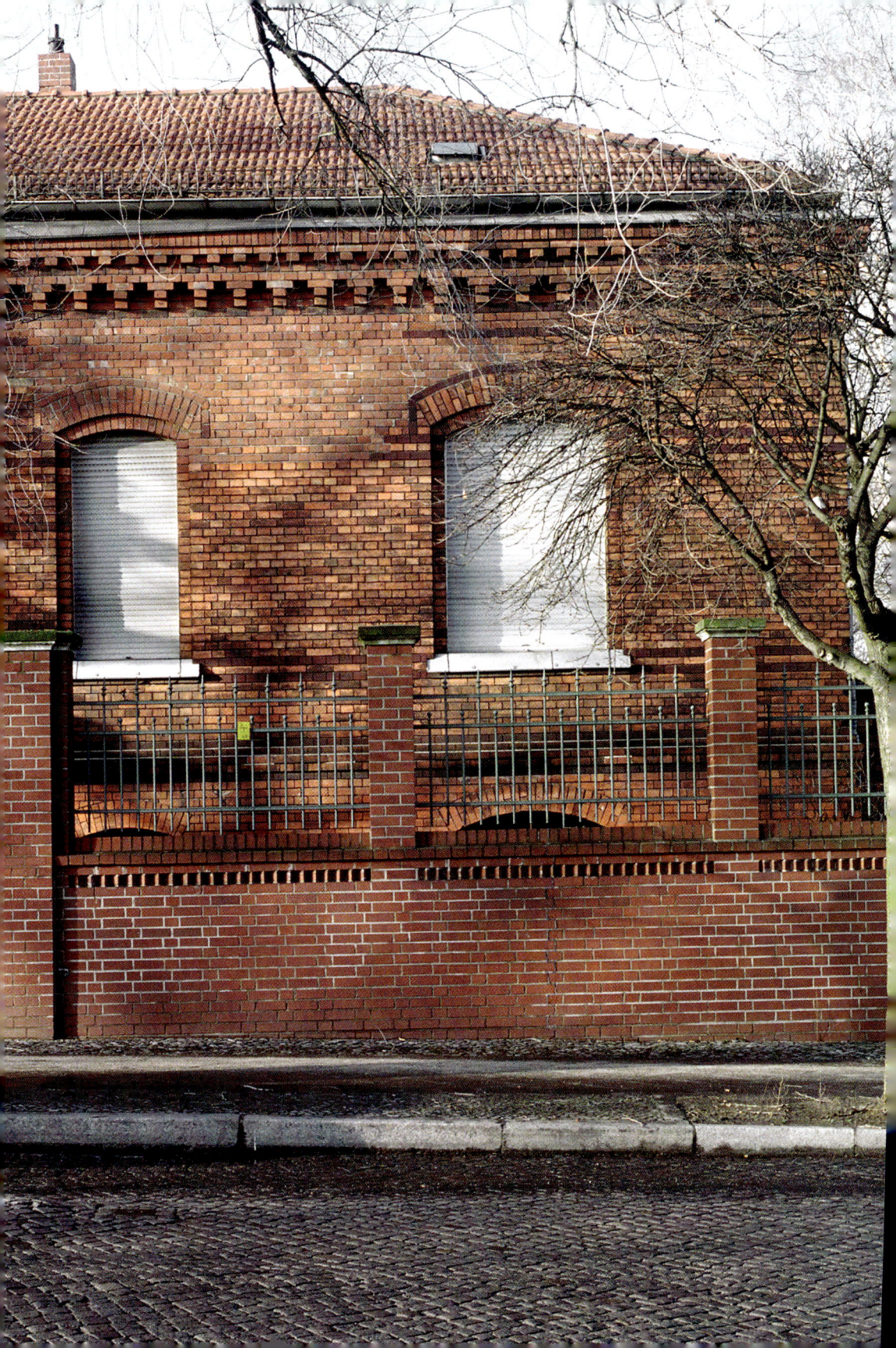

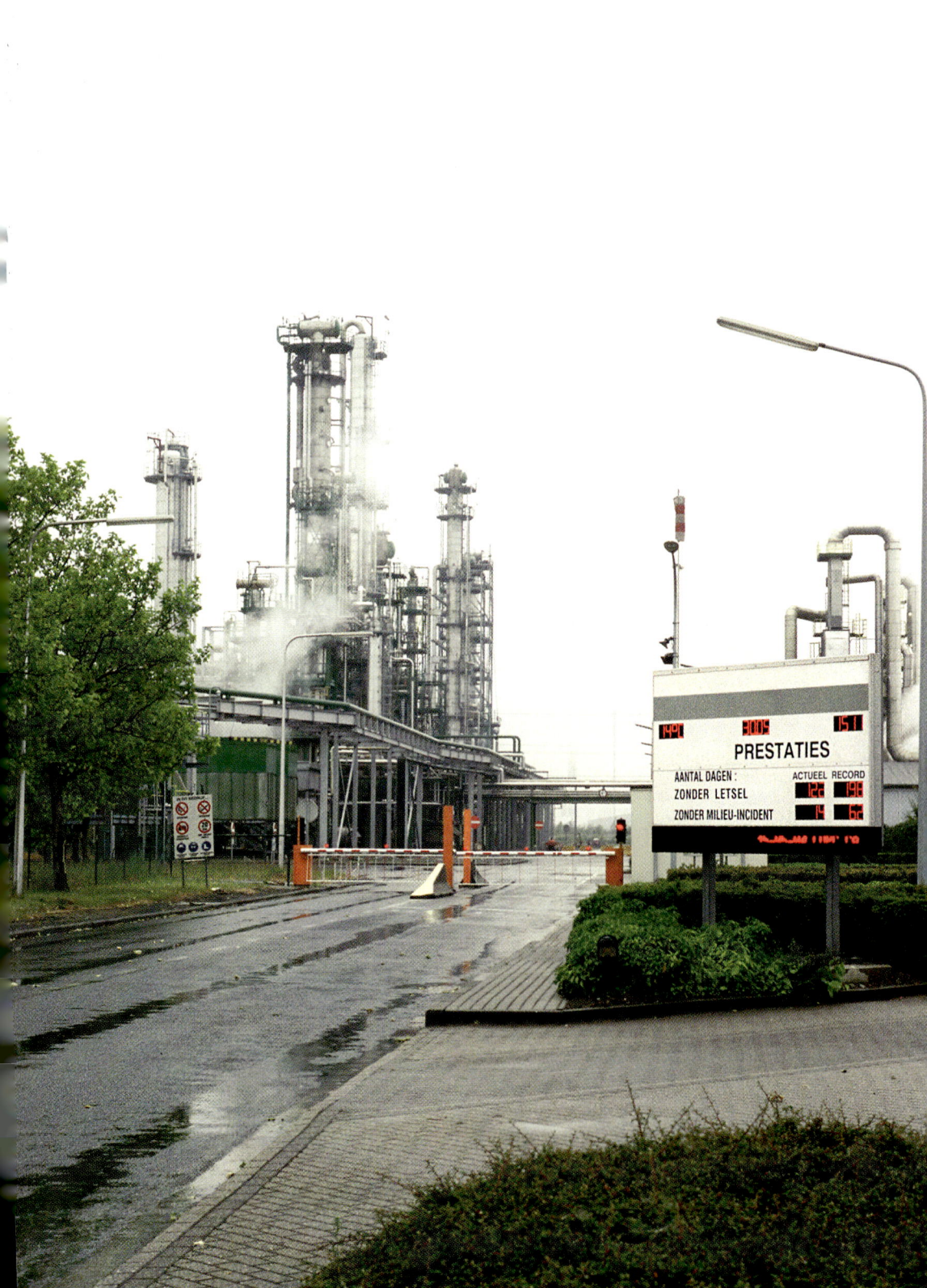

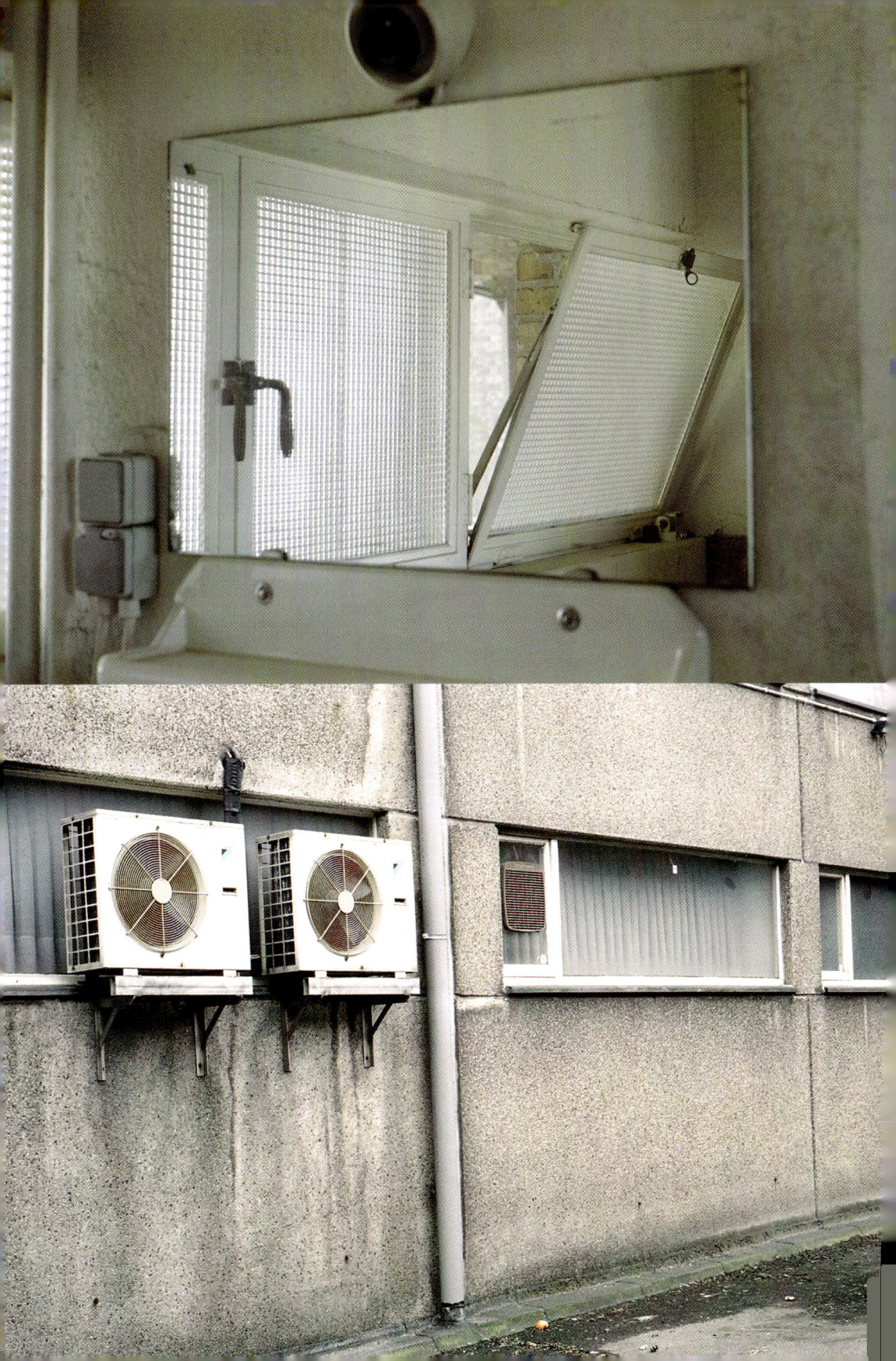

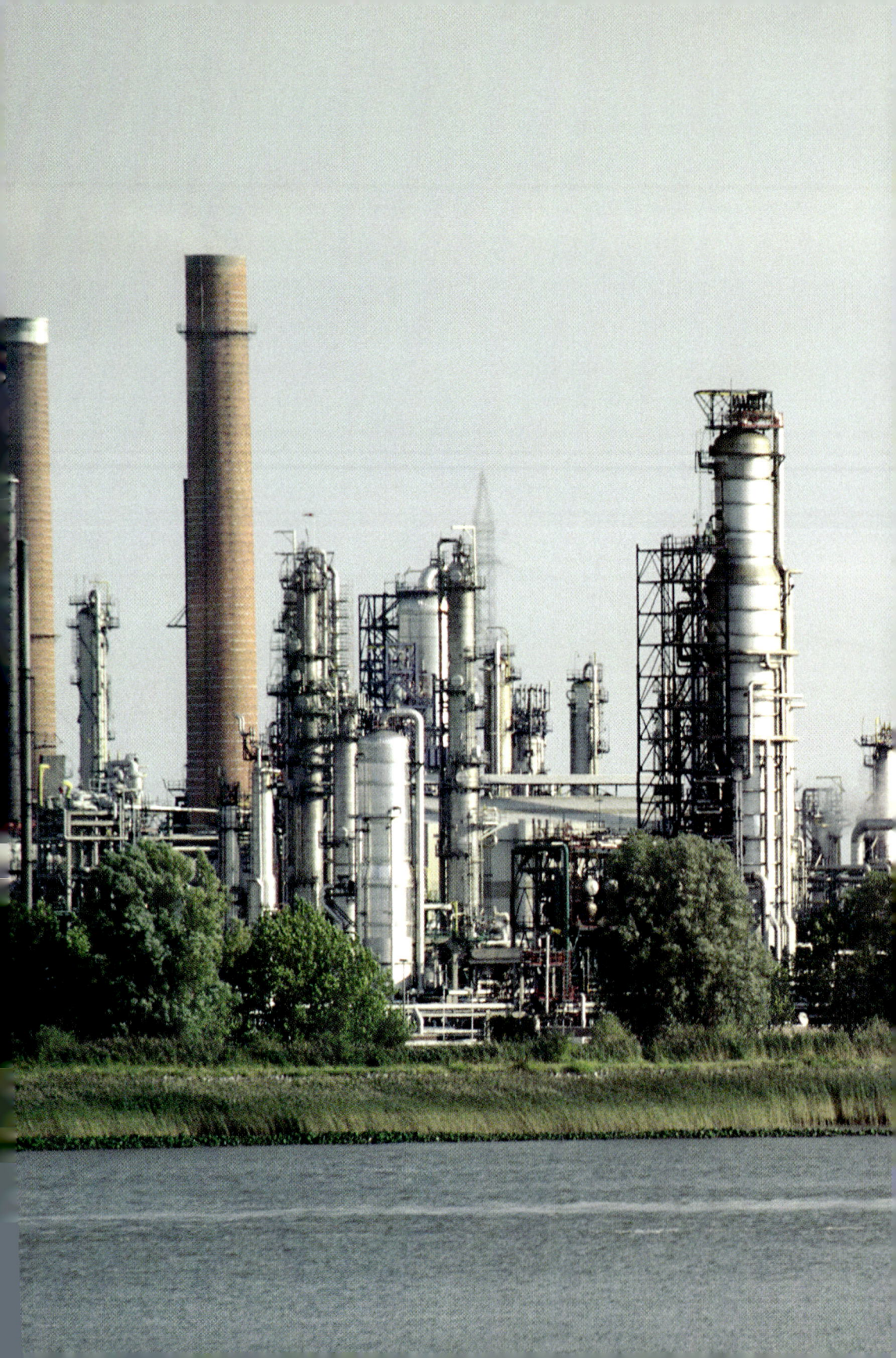

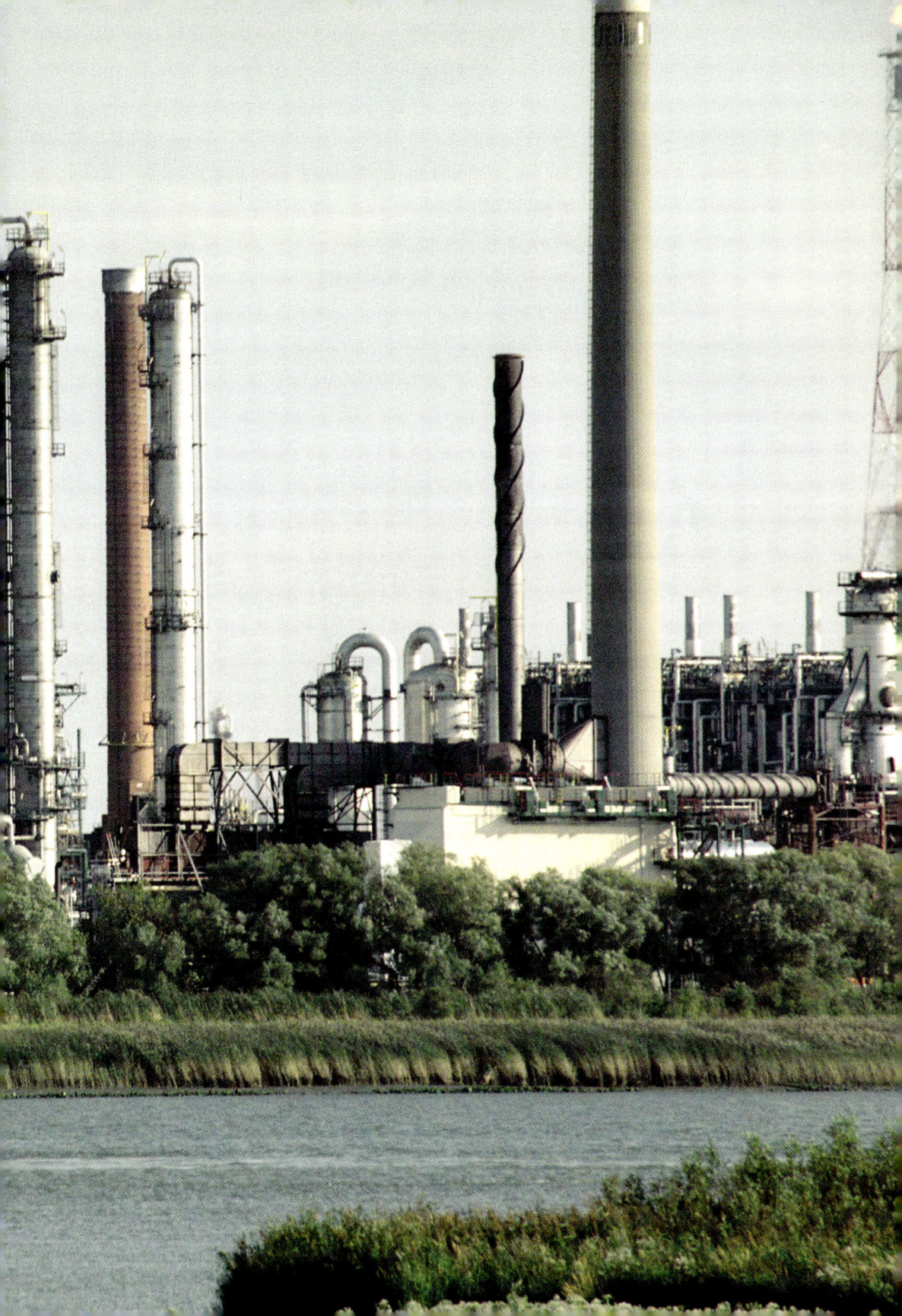

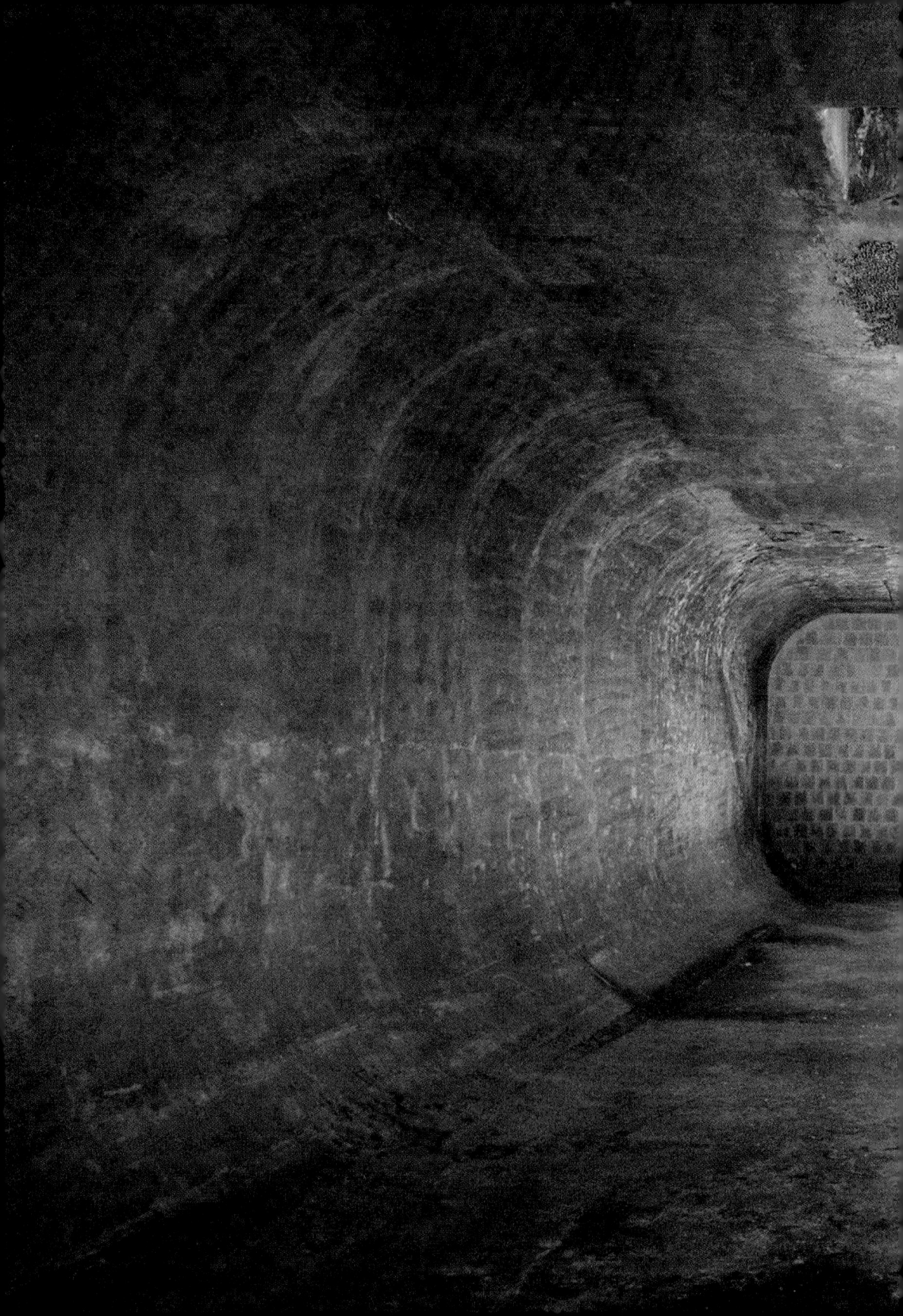

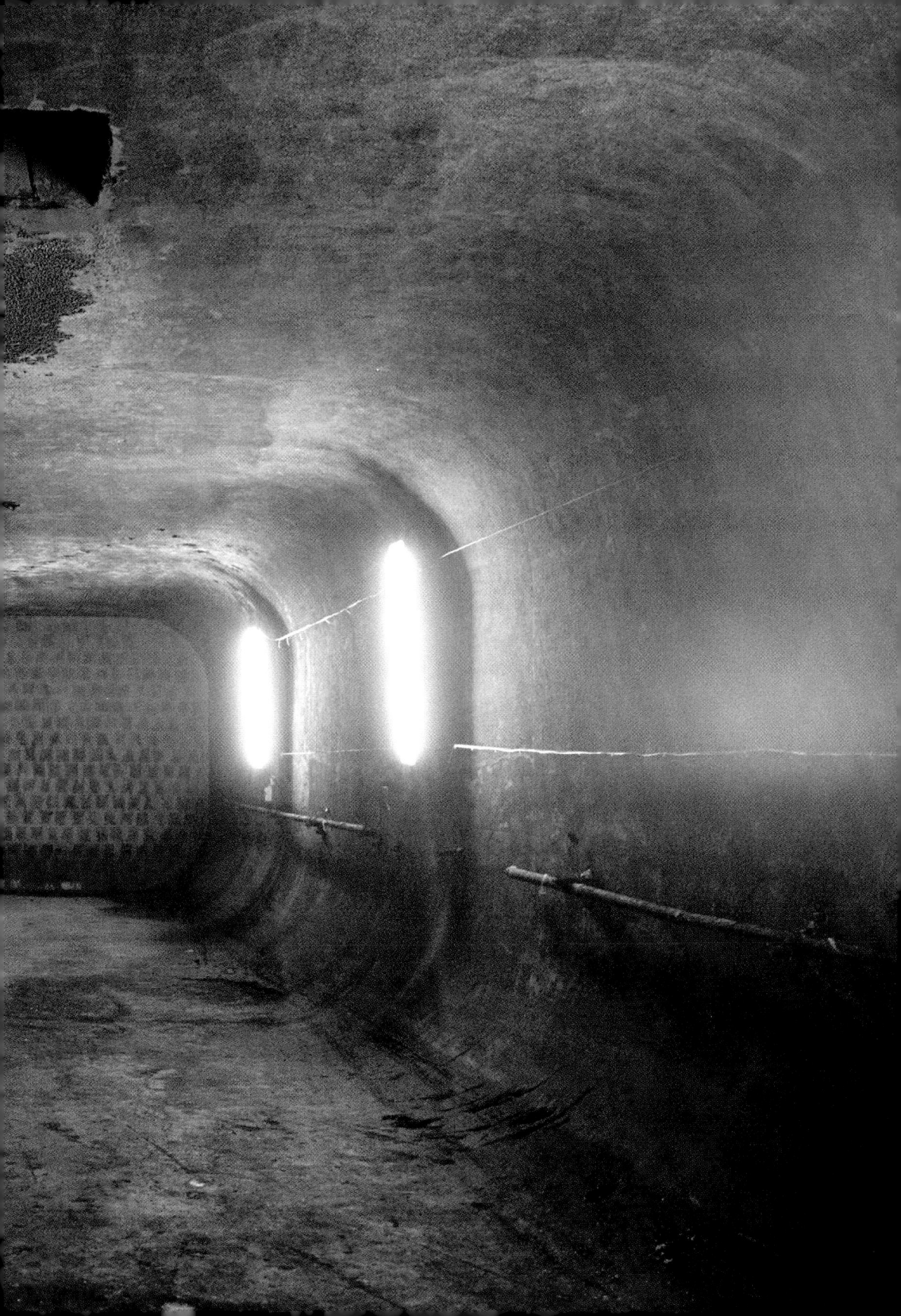

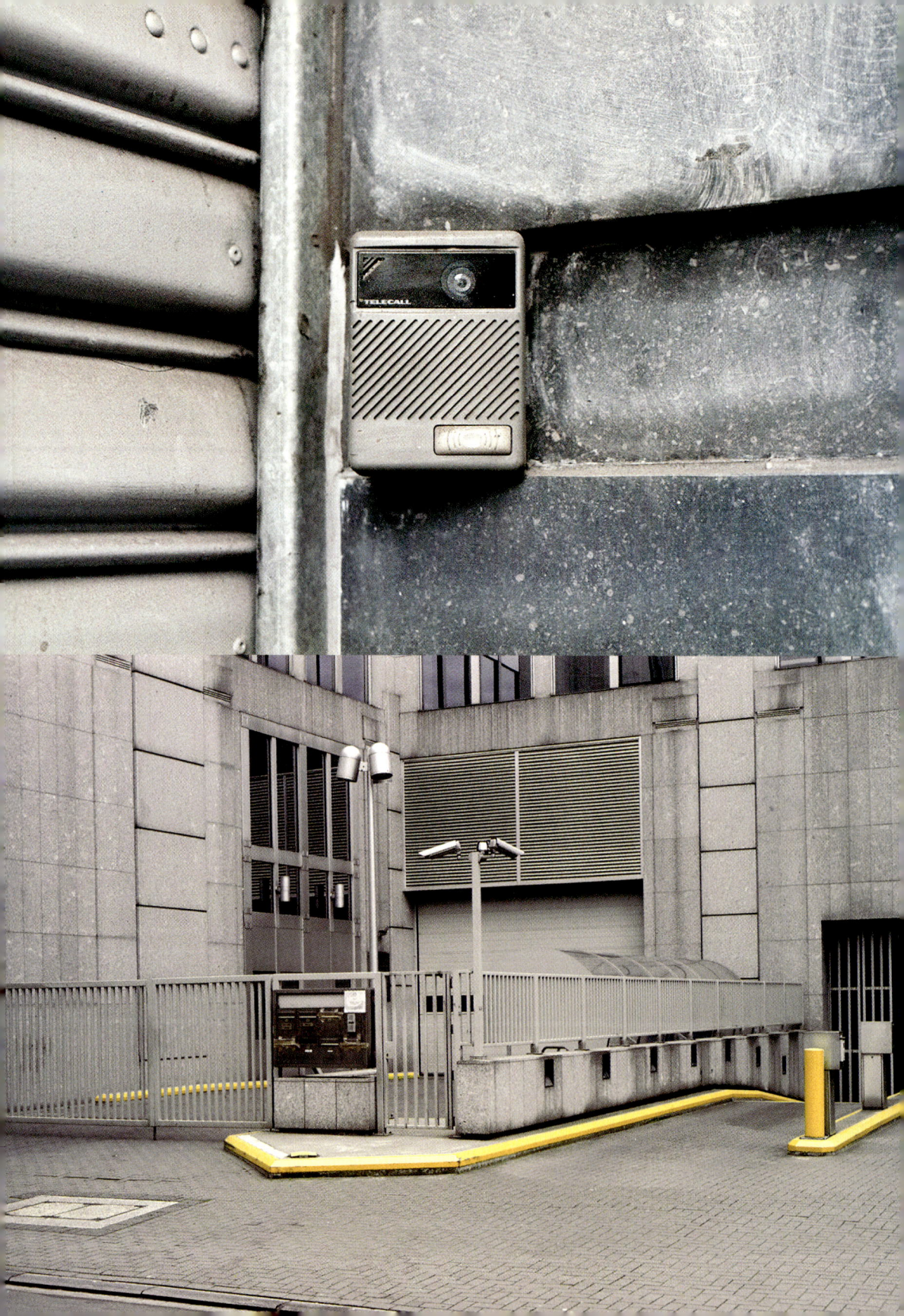

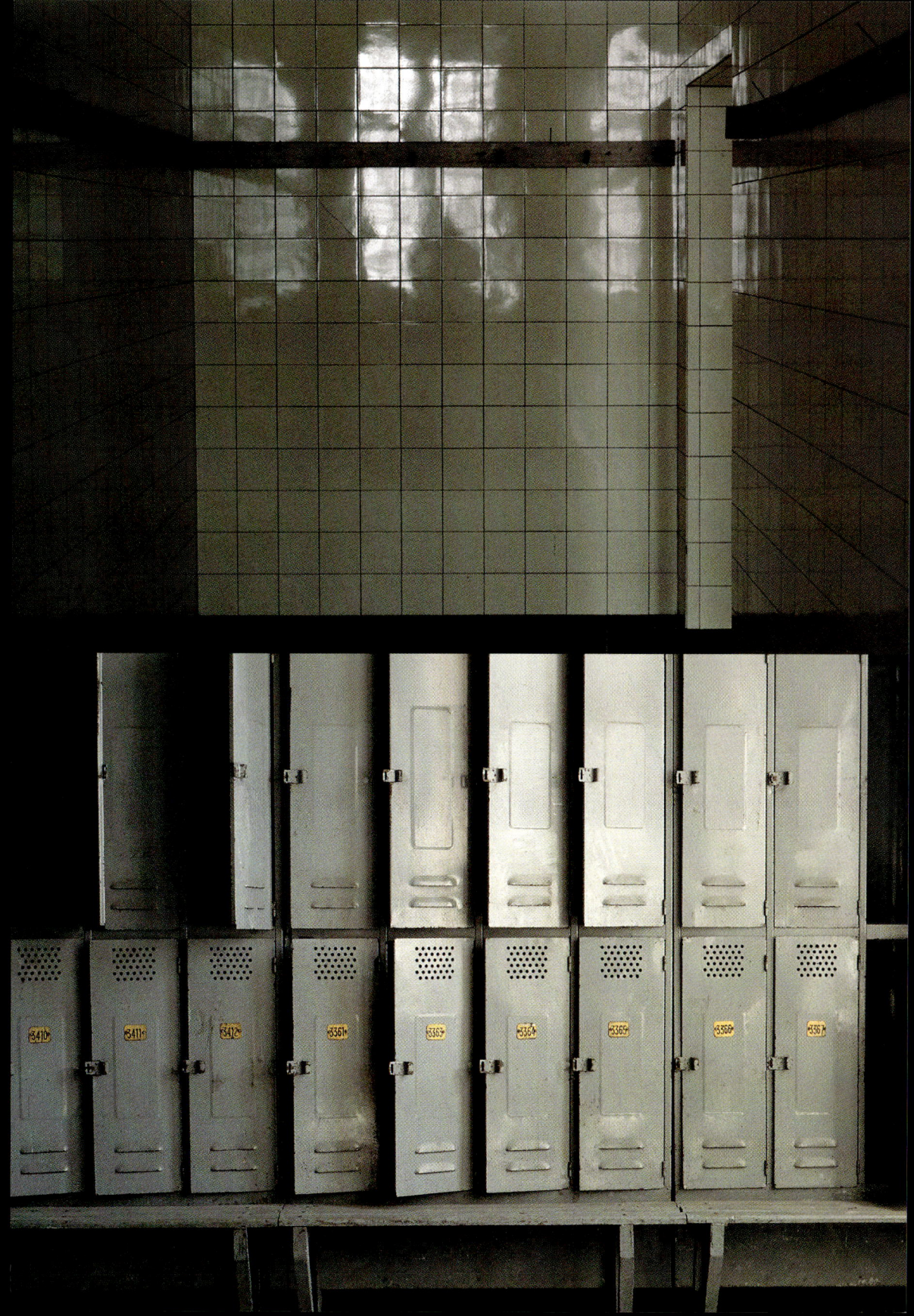

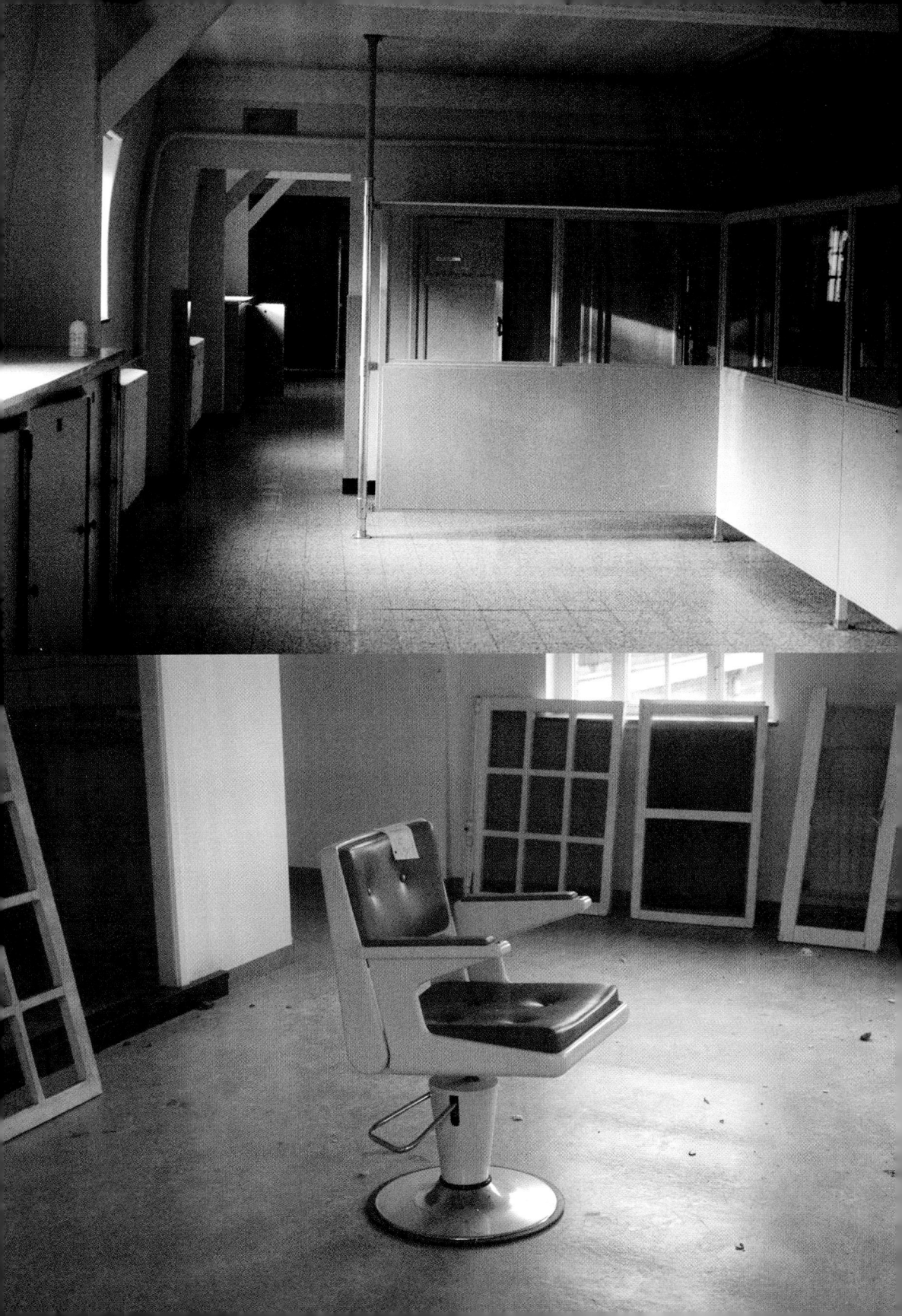

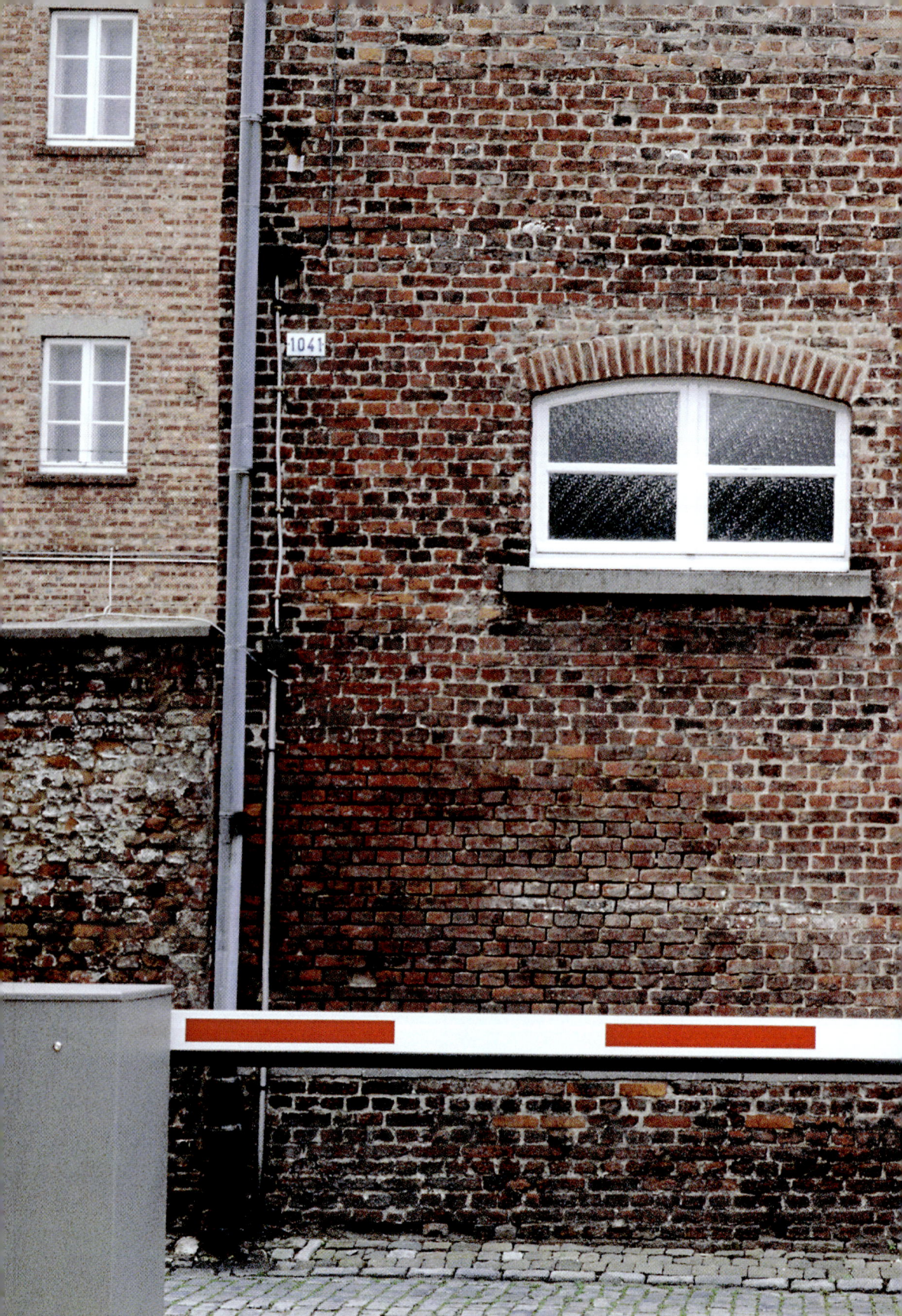

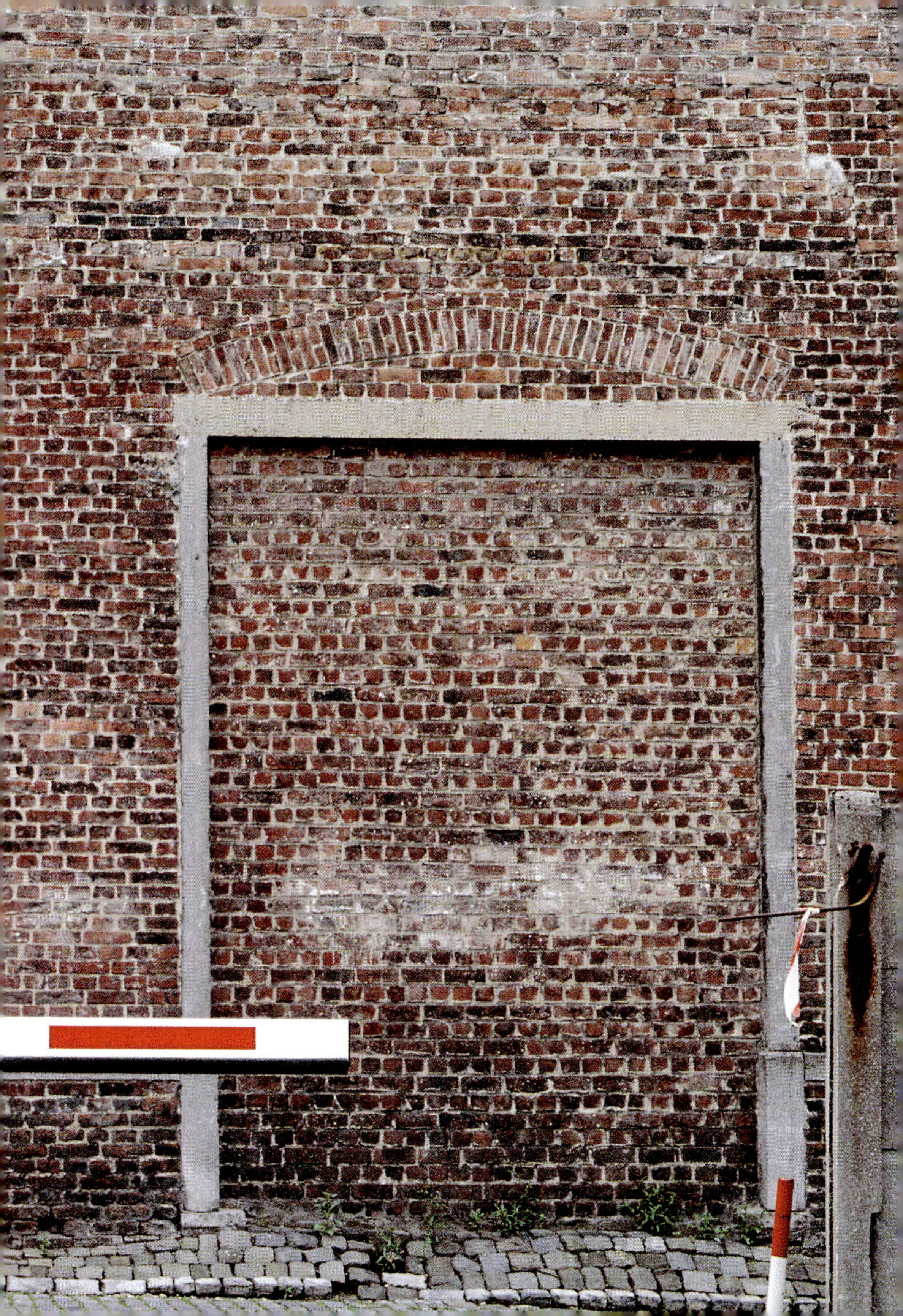

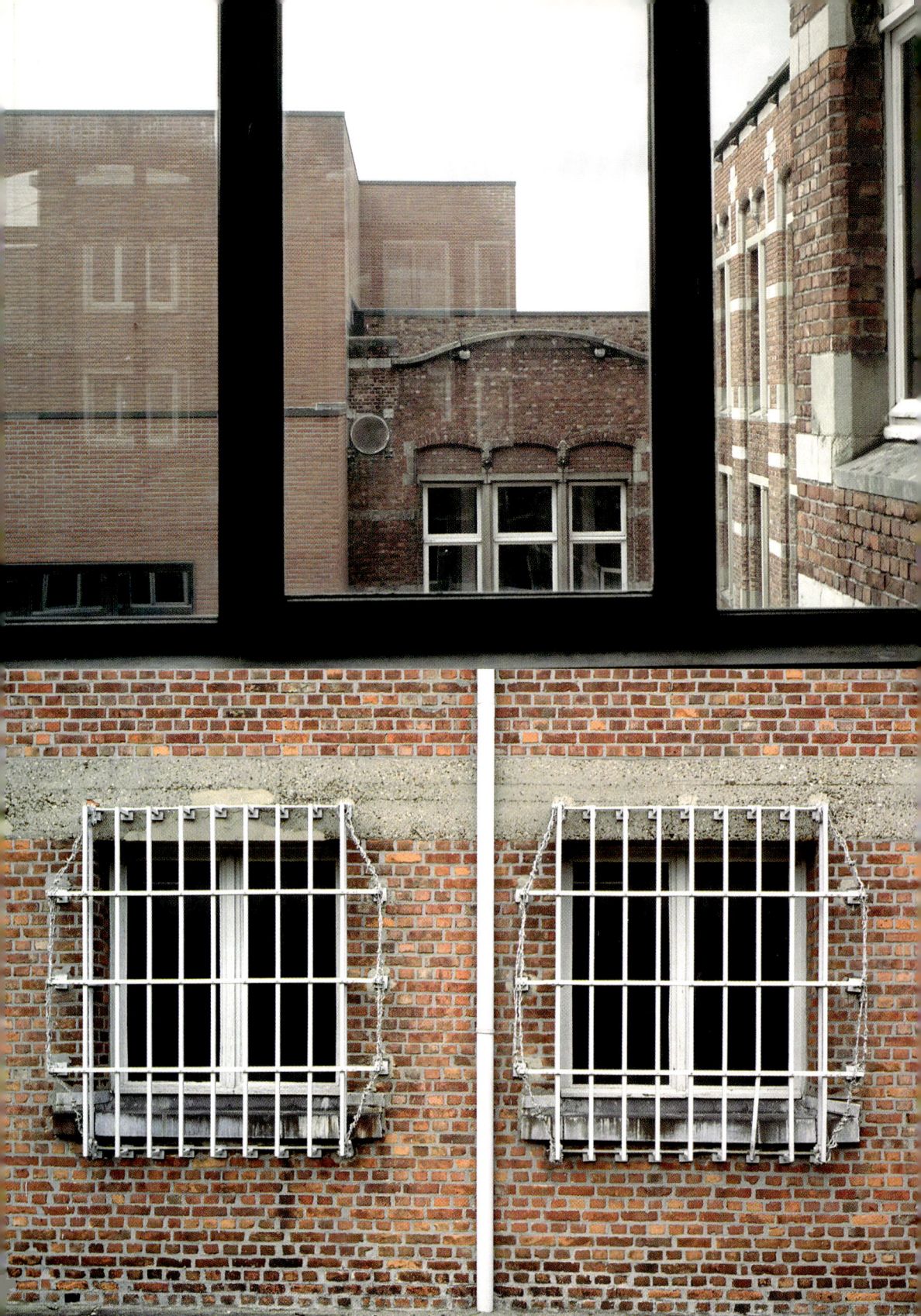

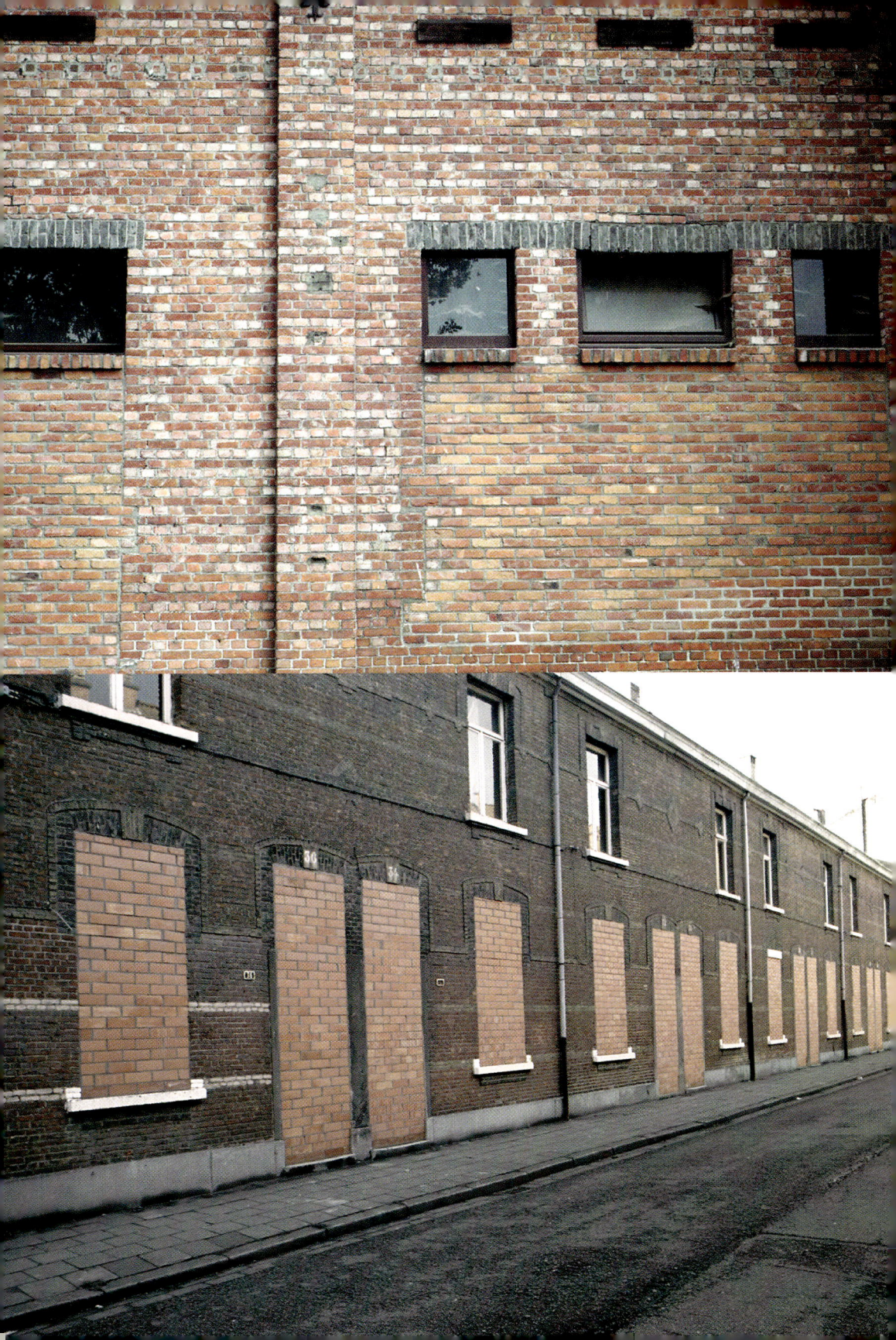

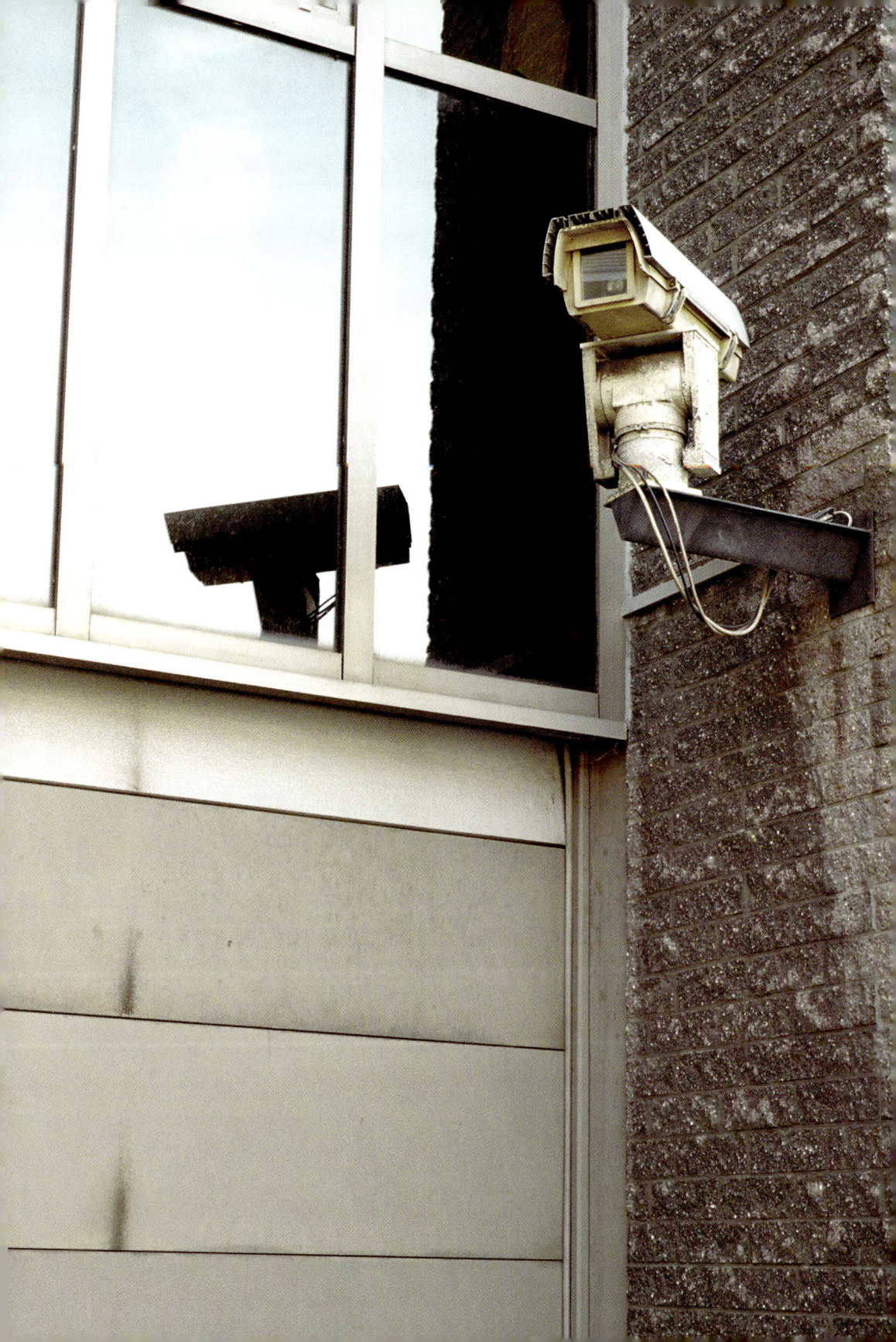

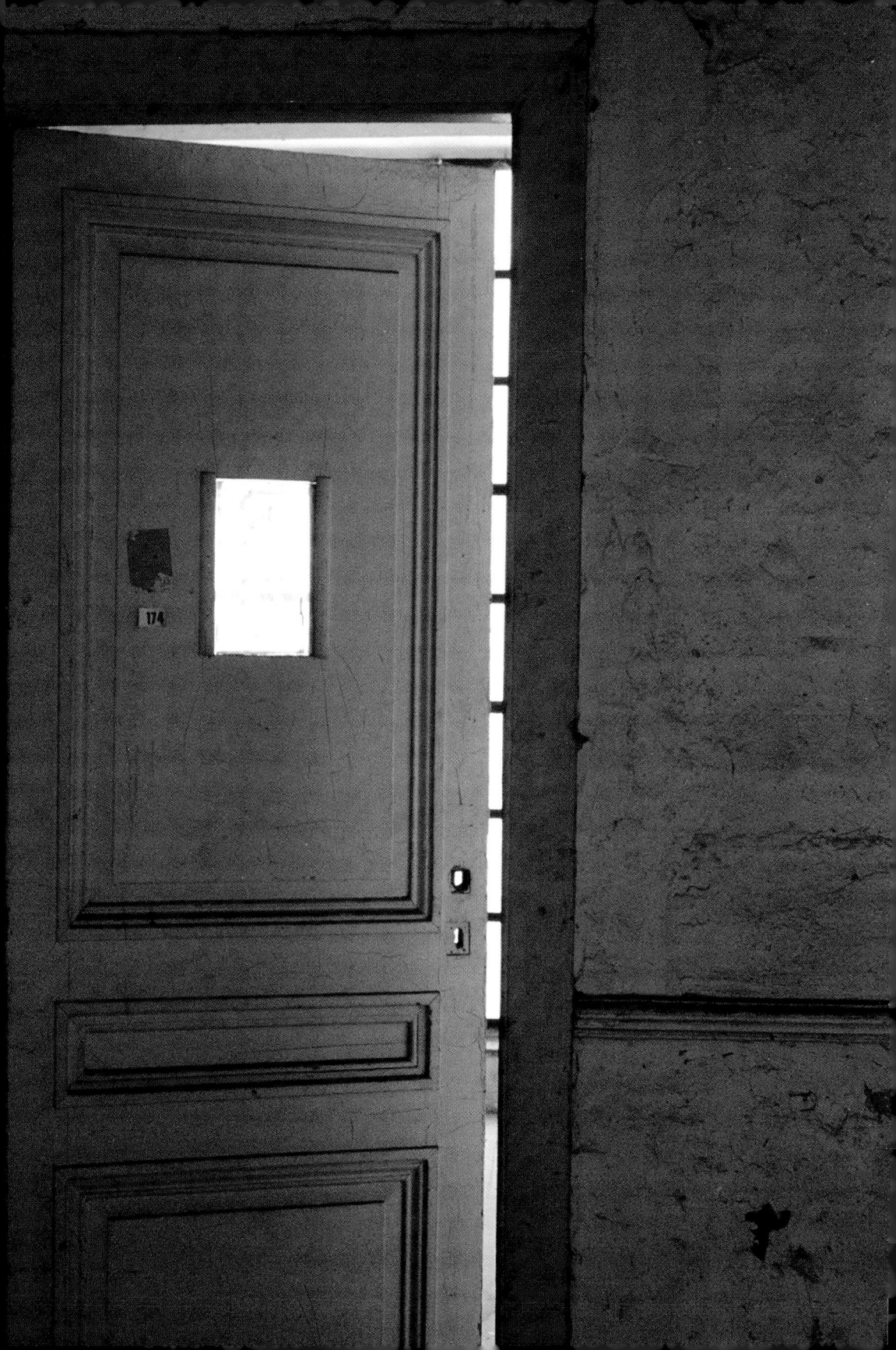

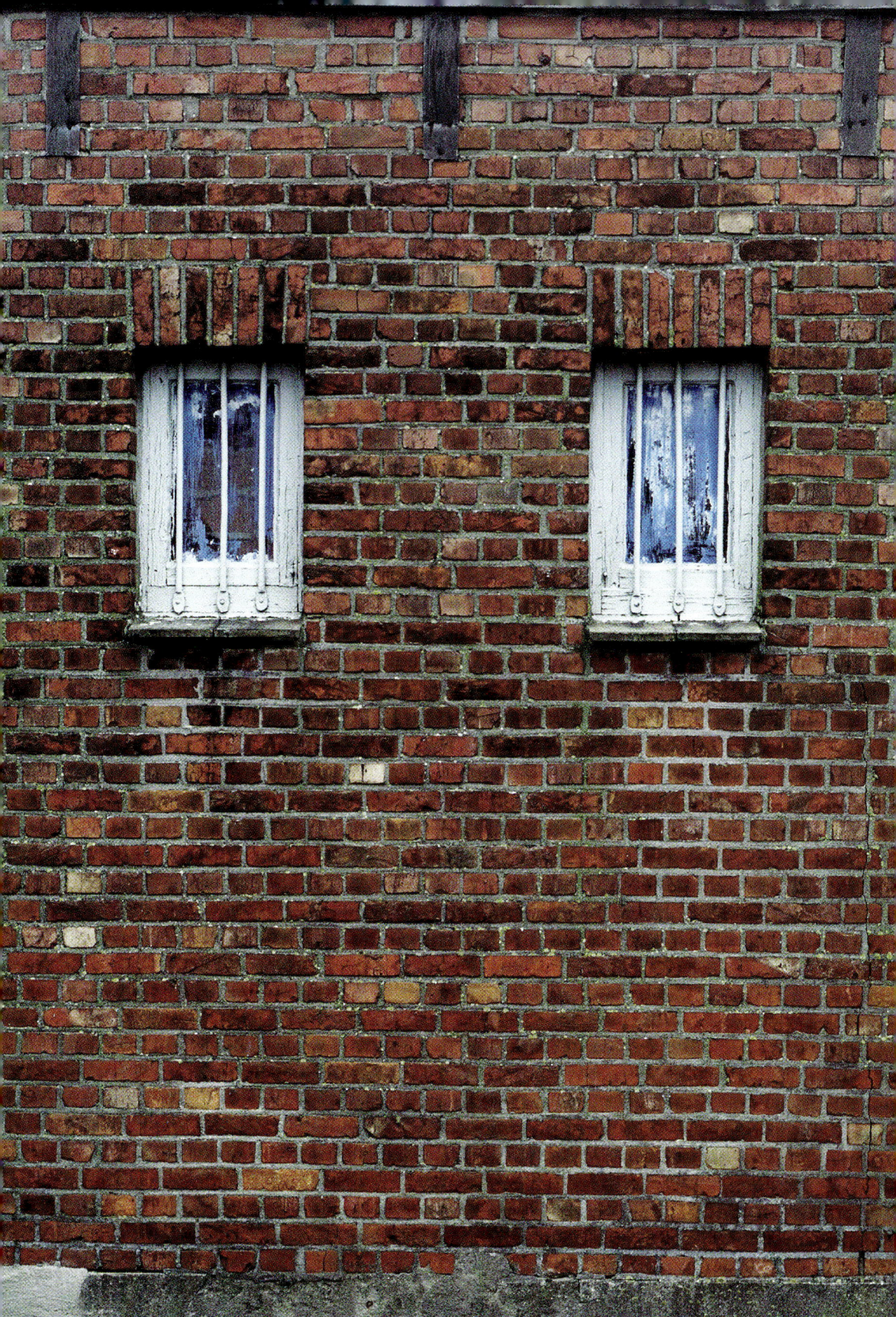

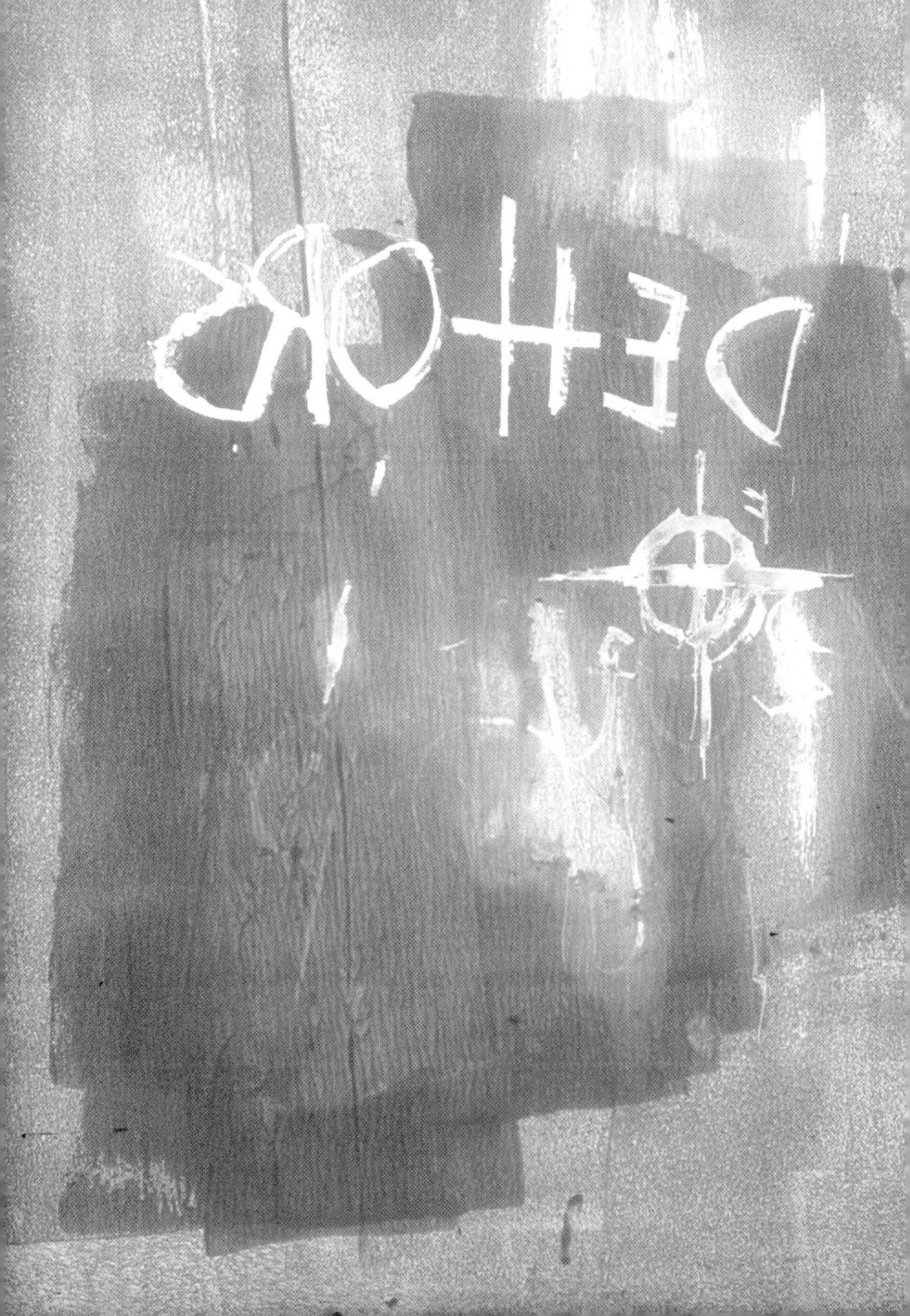

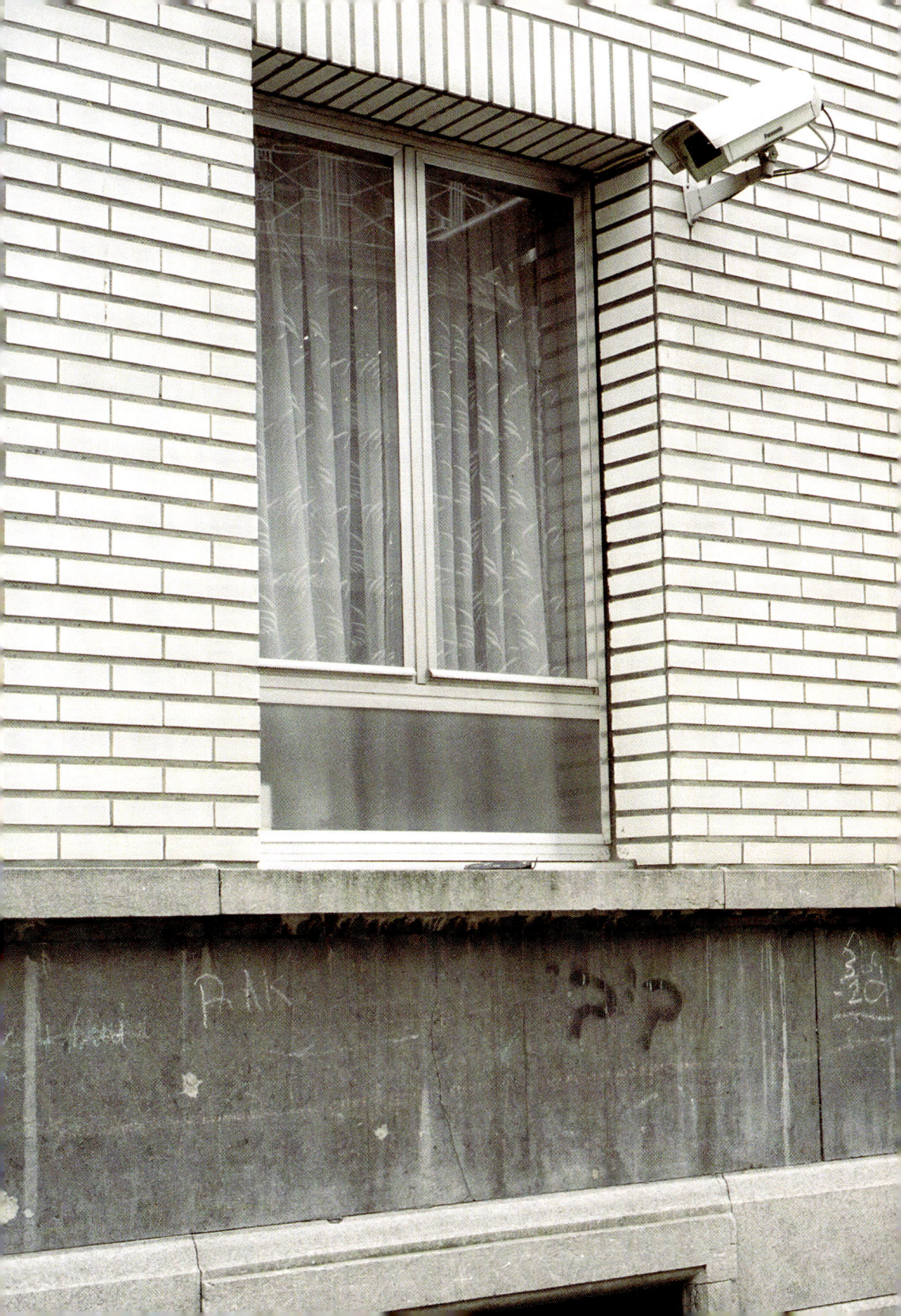

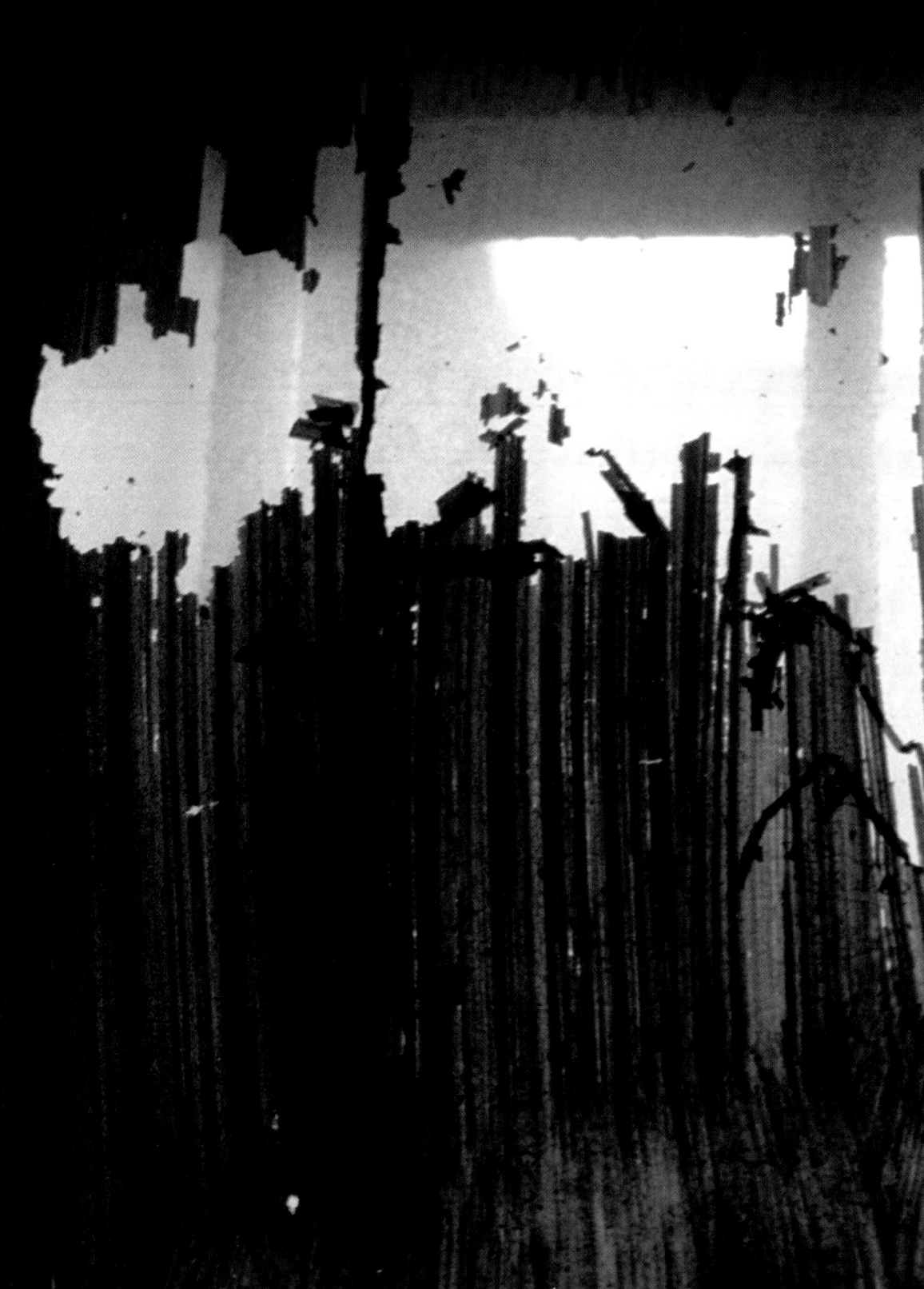

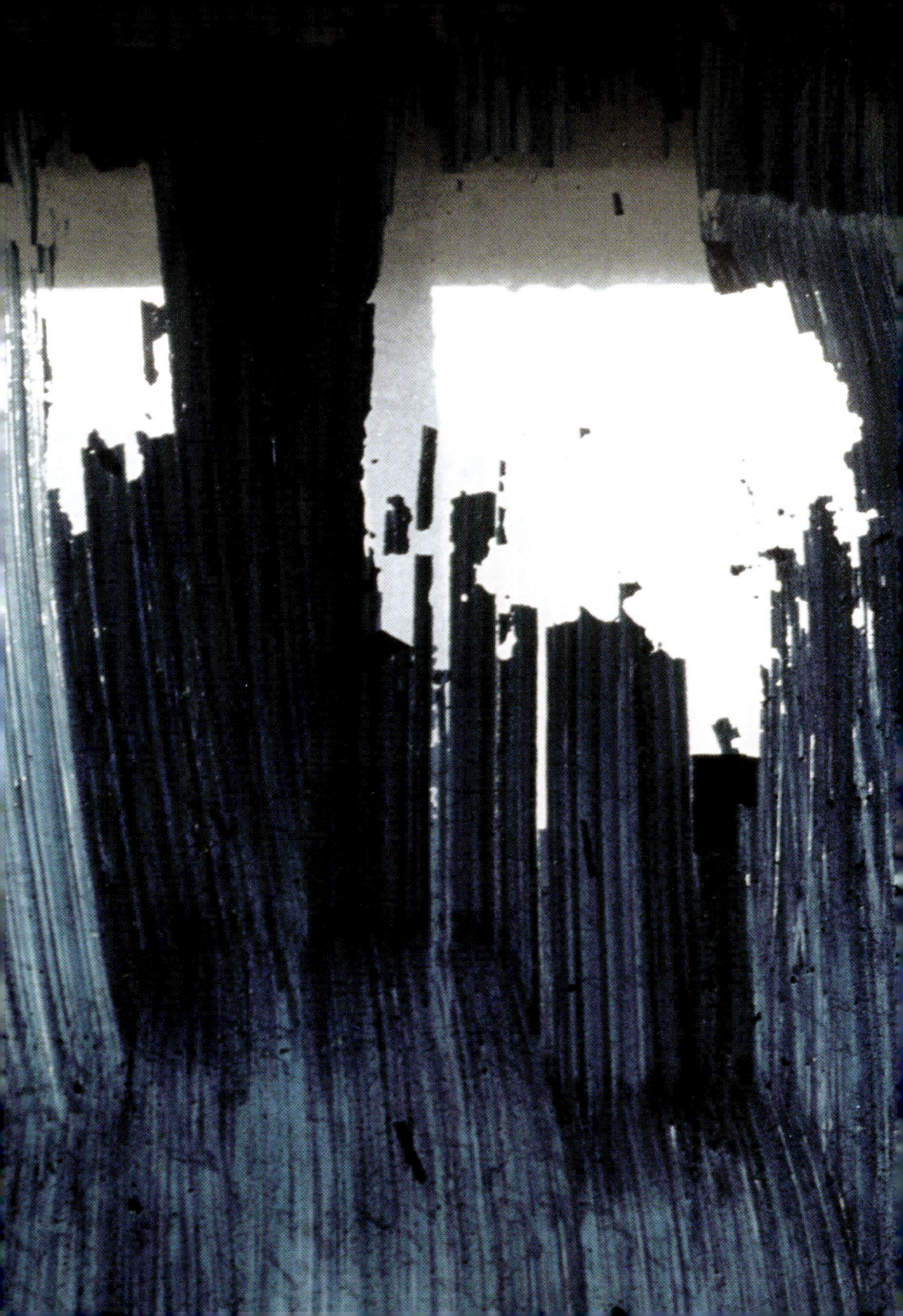

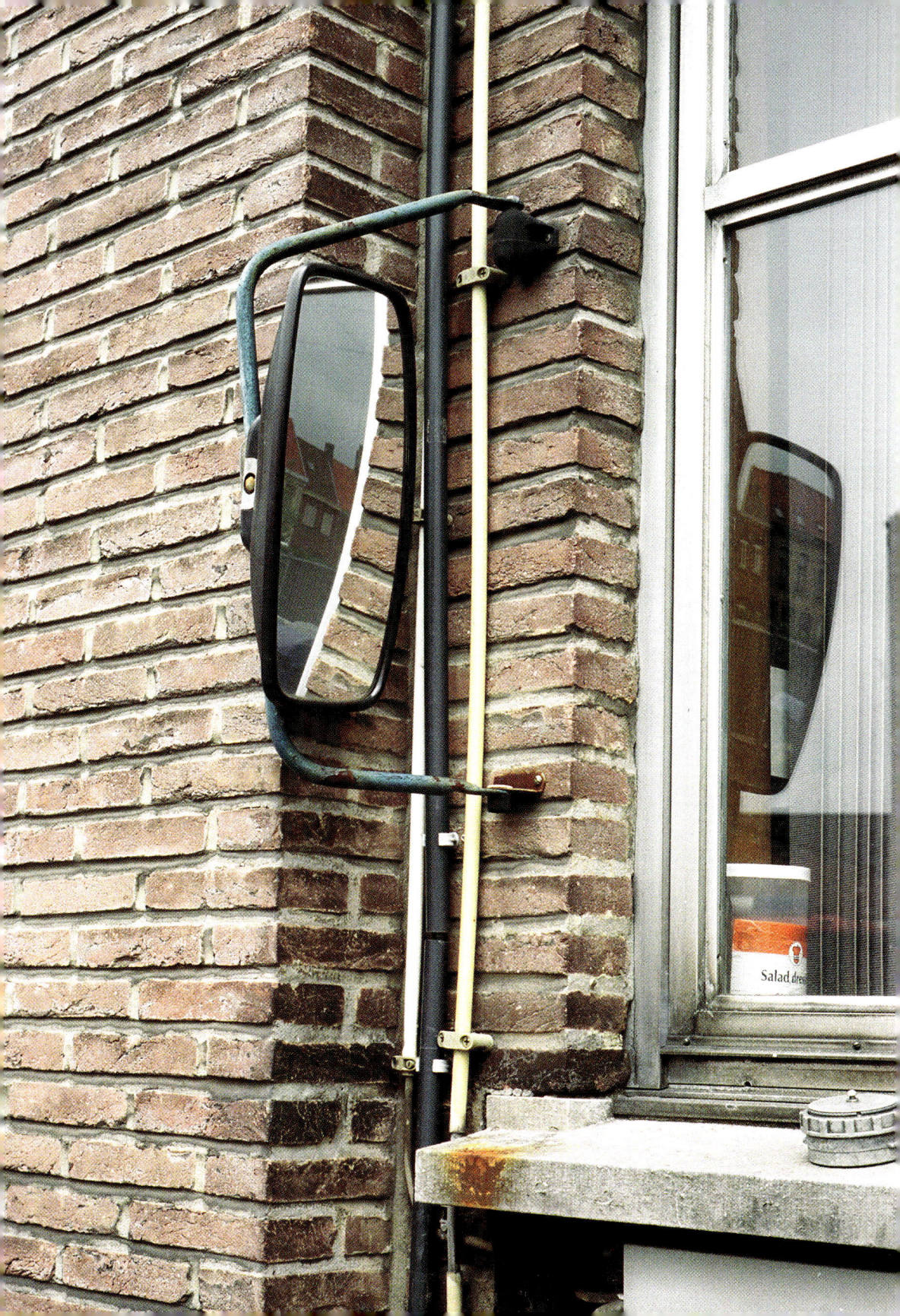

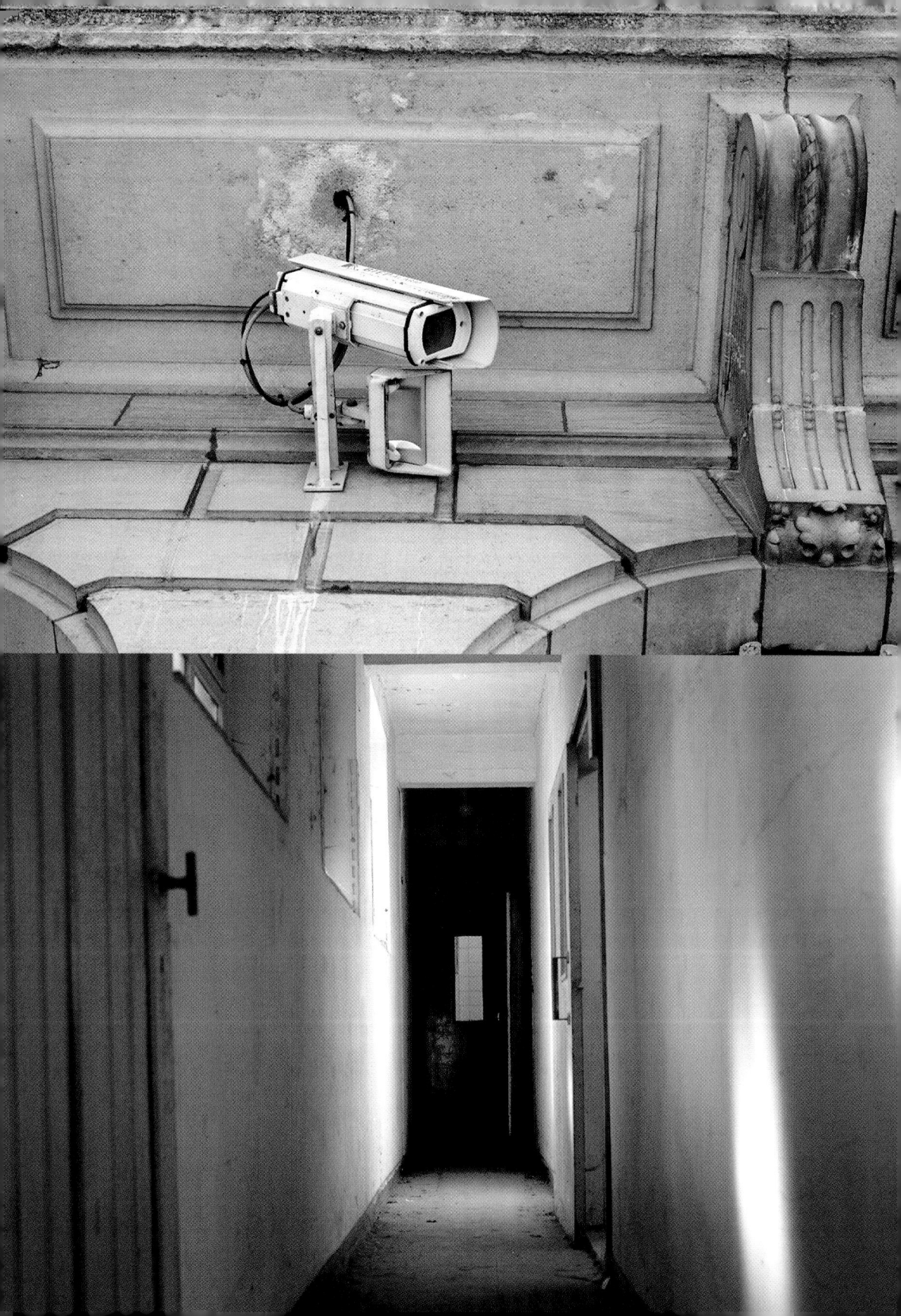

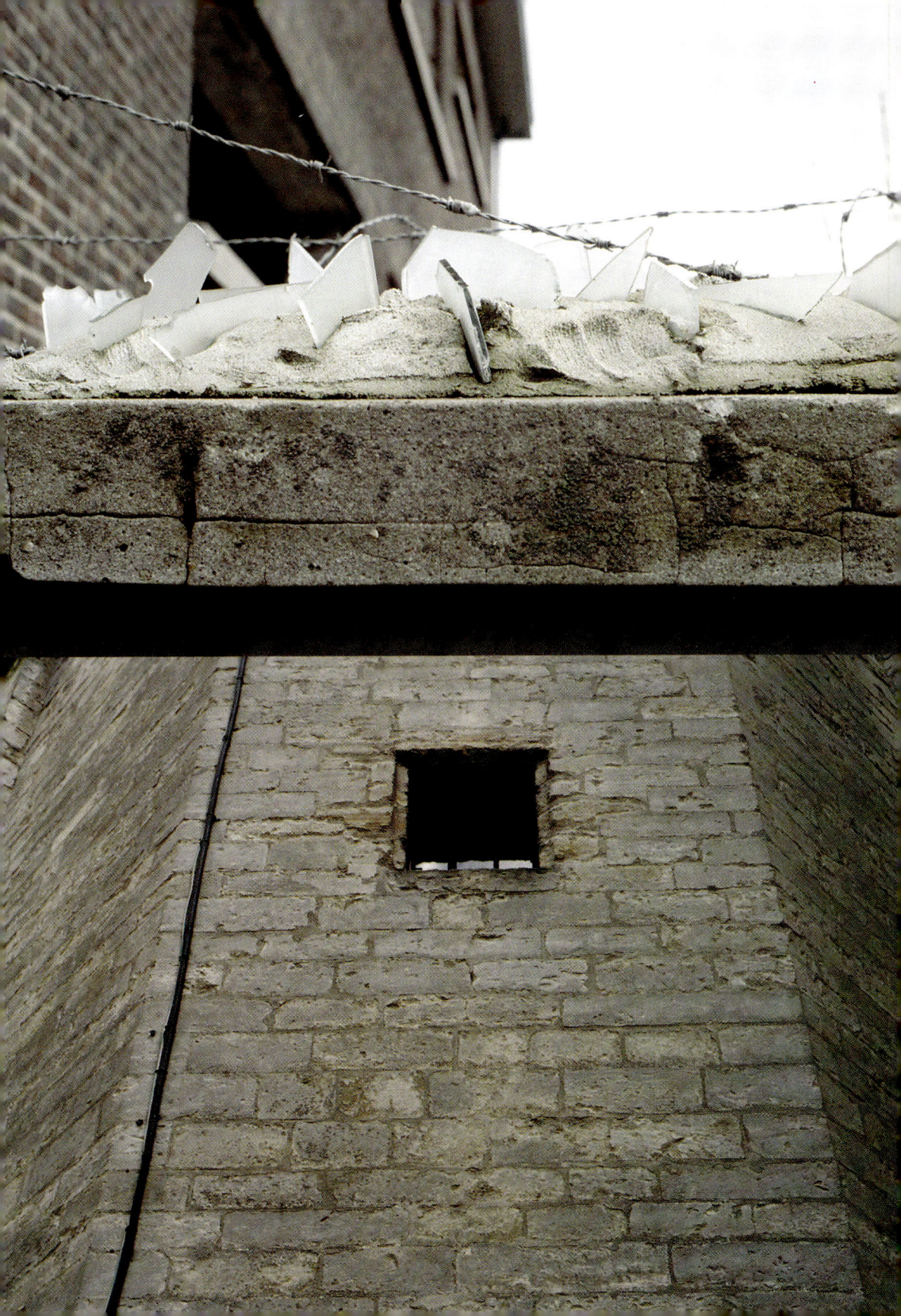

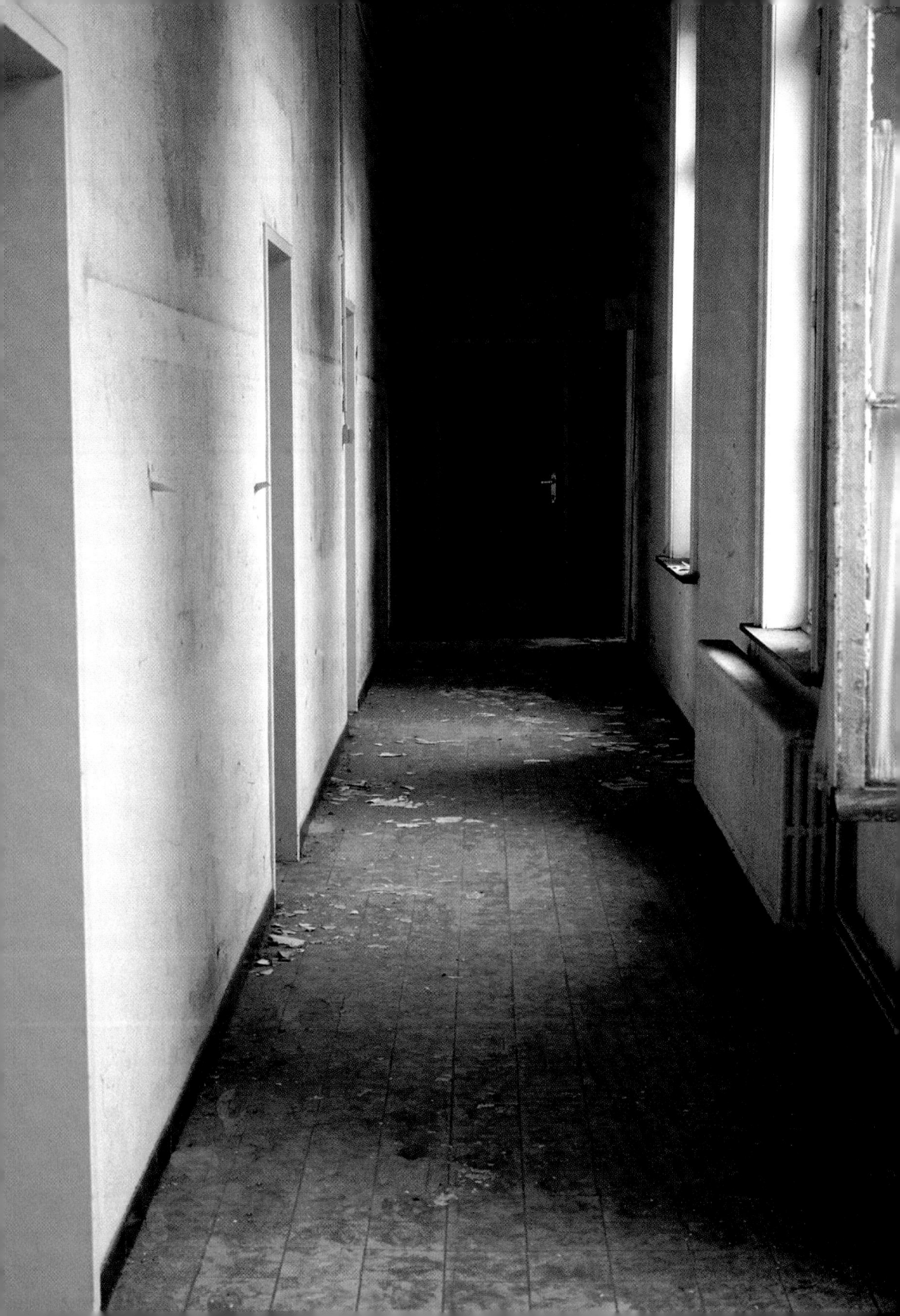

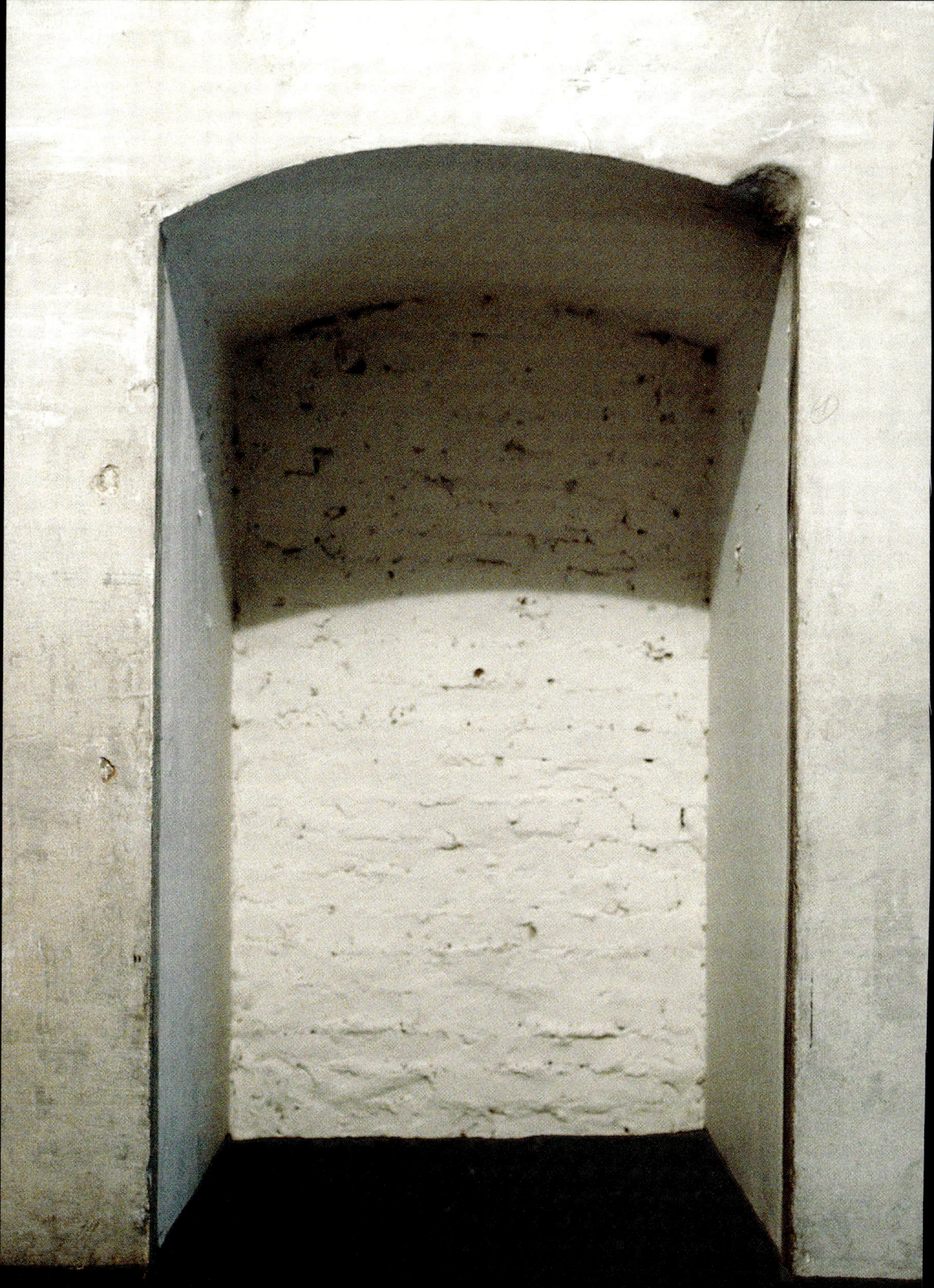

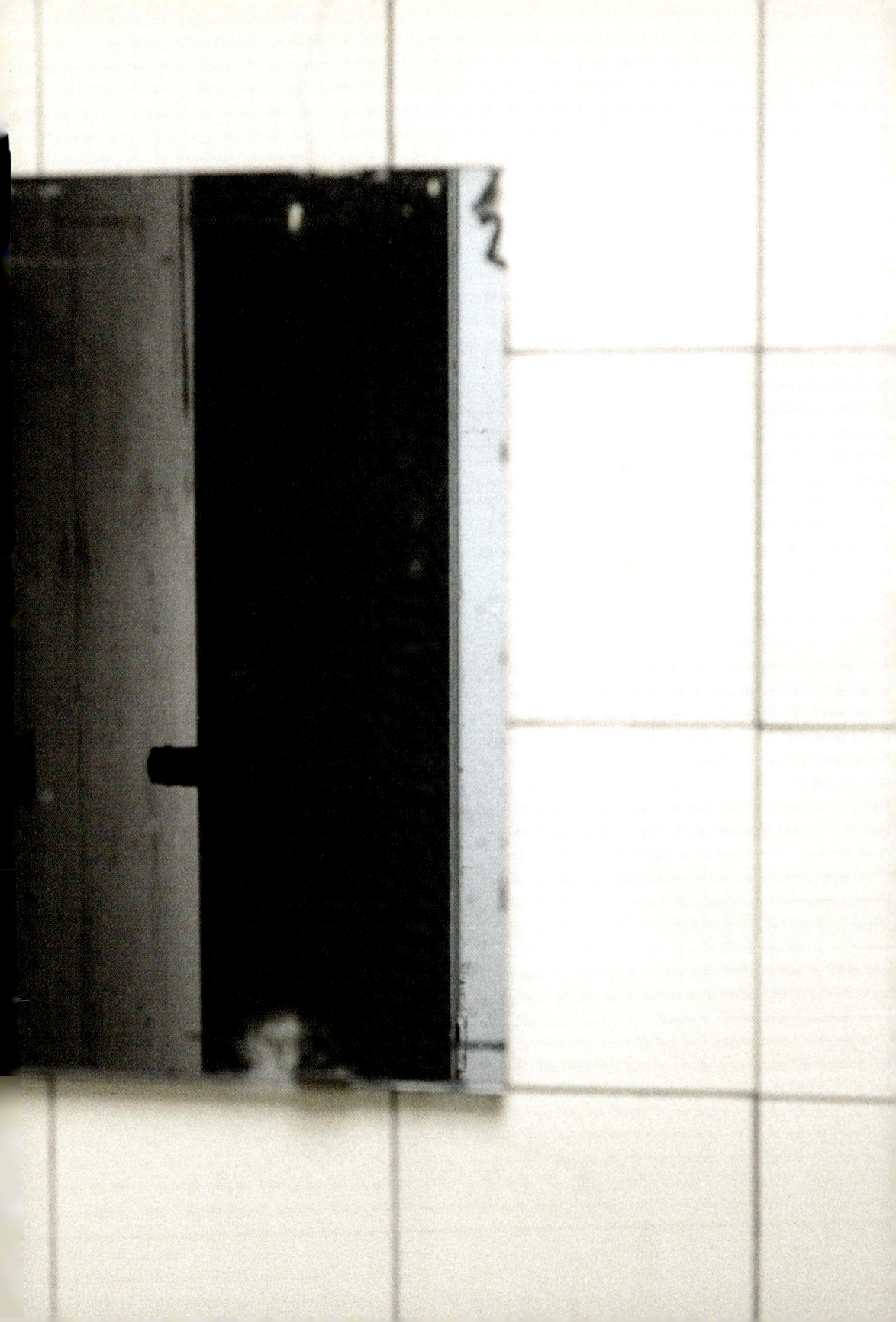

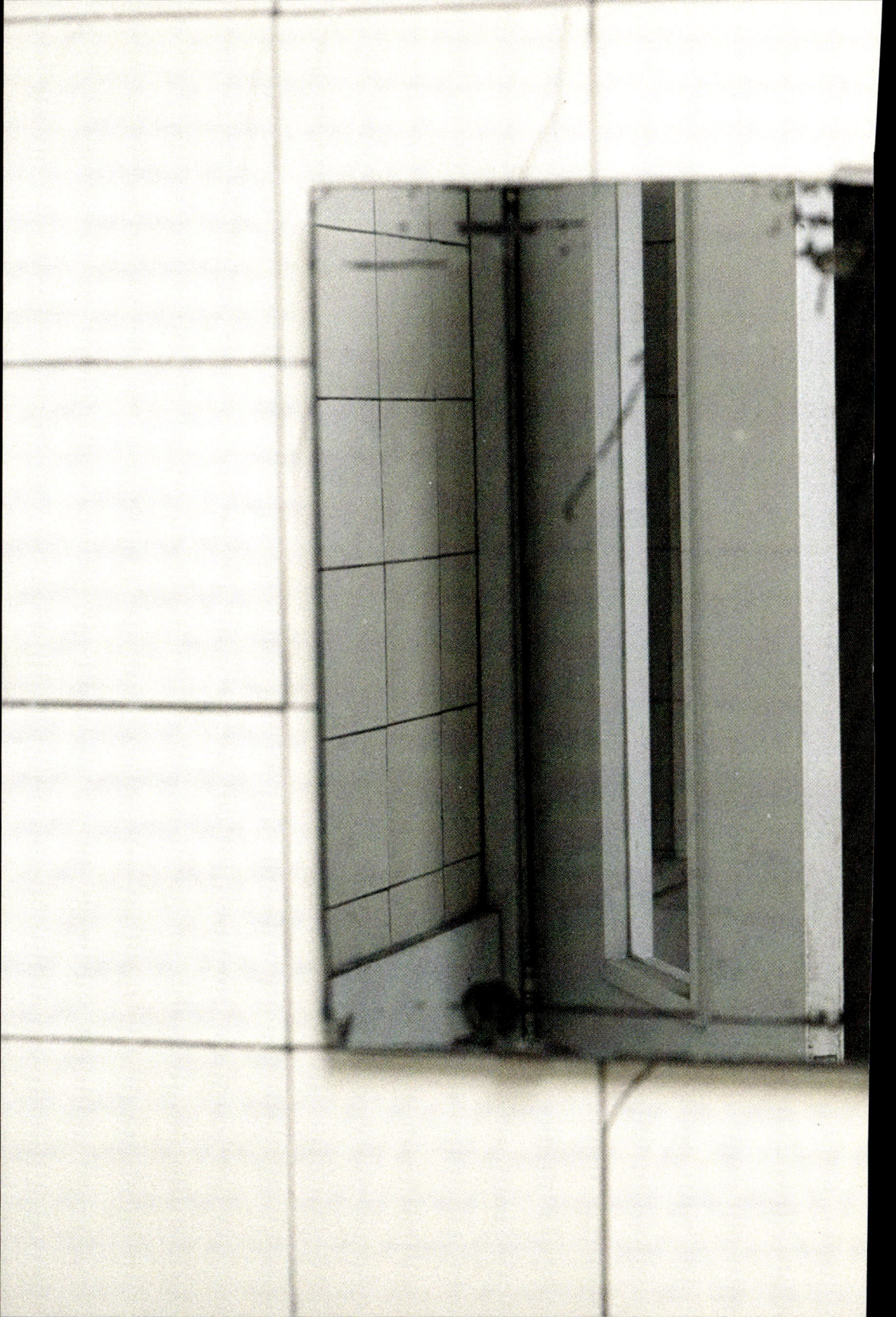

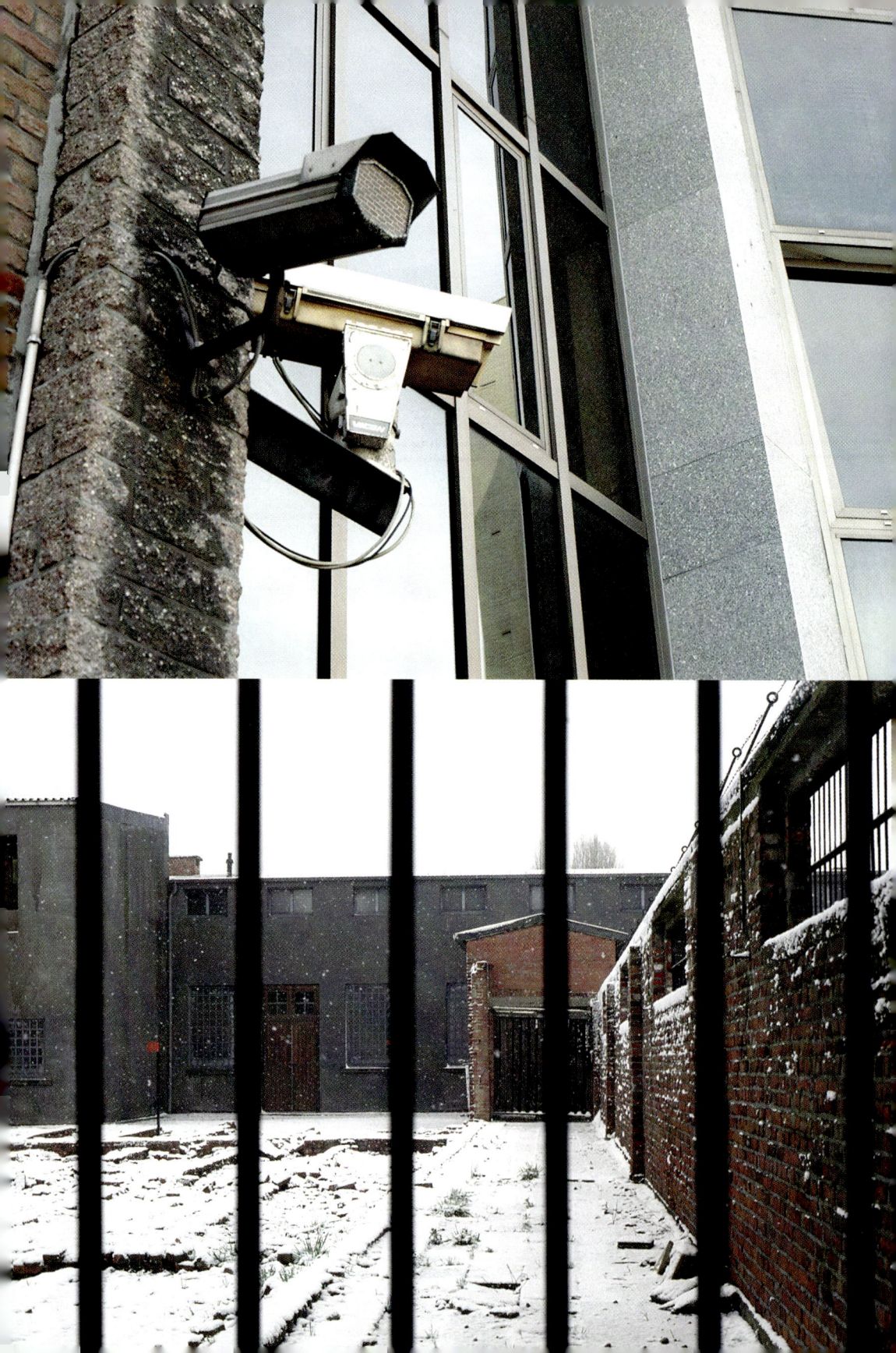

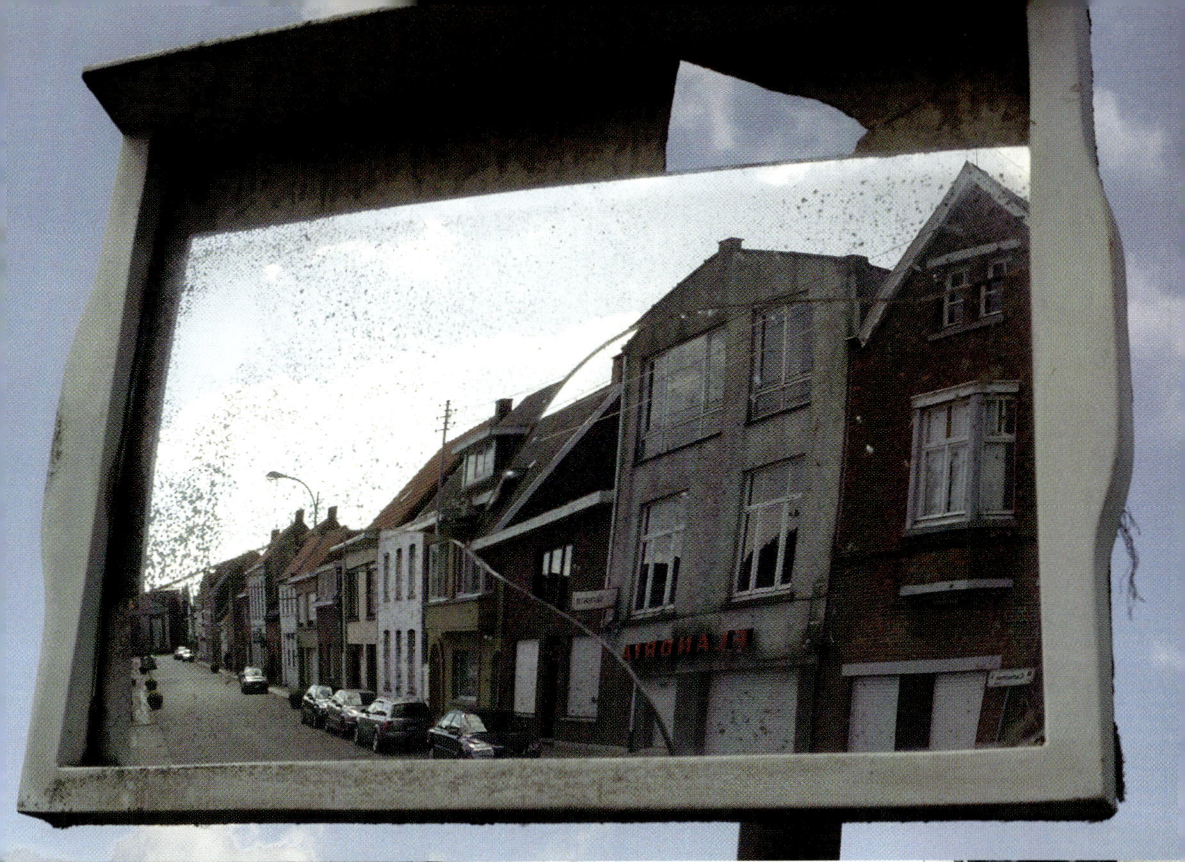

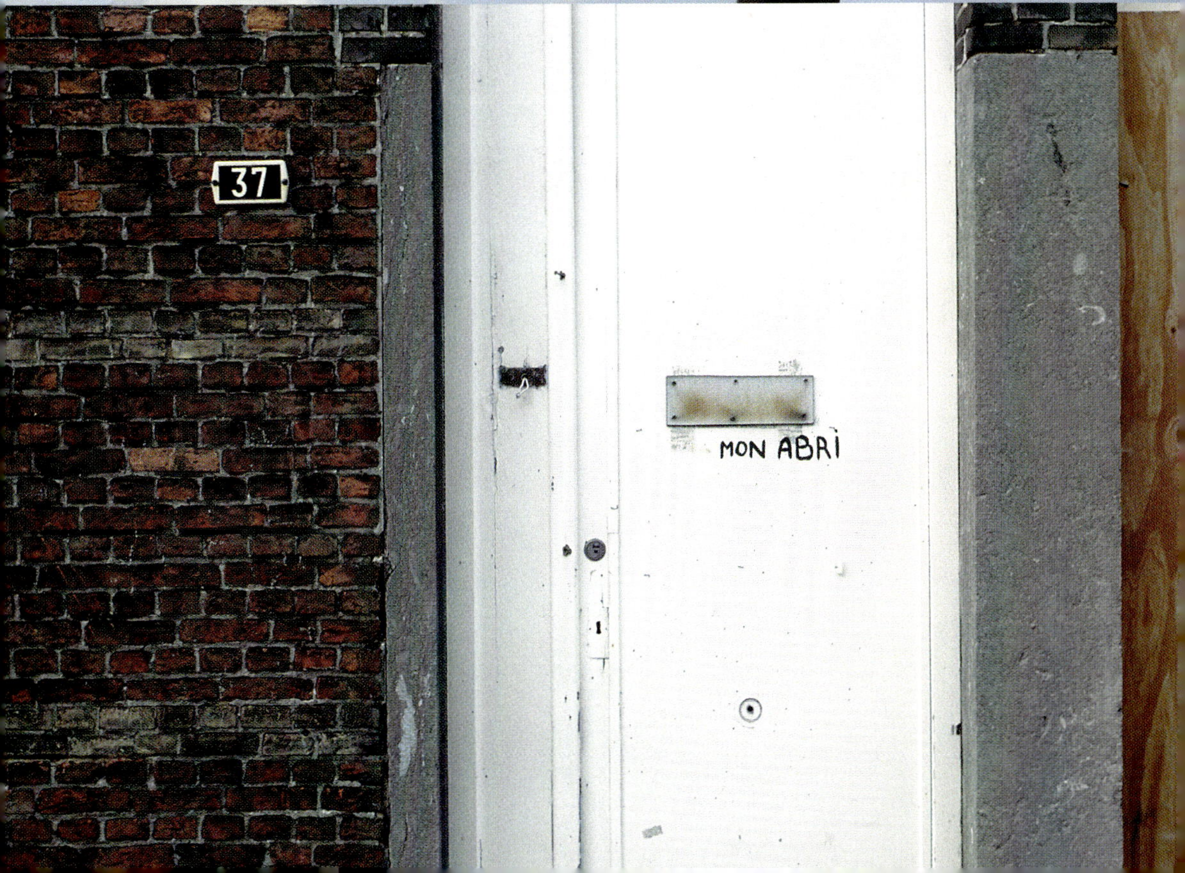

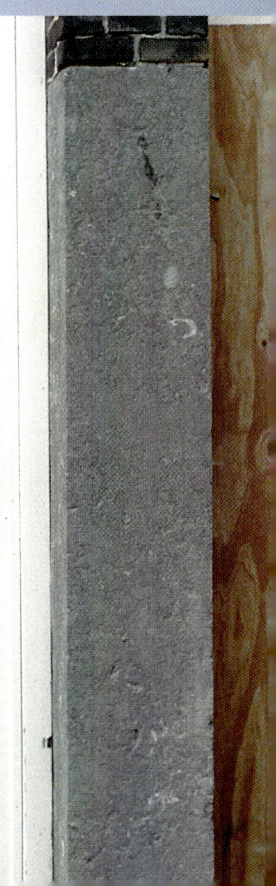

MON ABRI

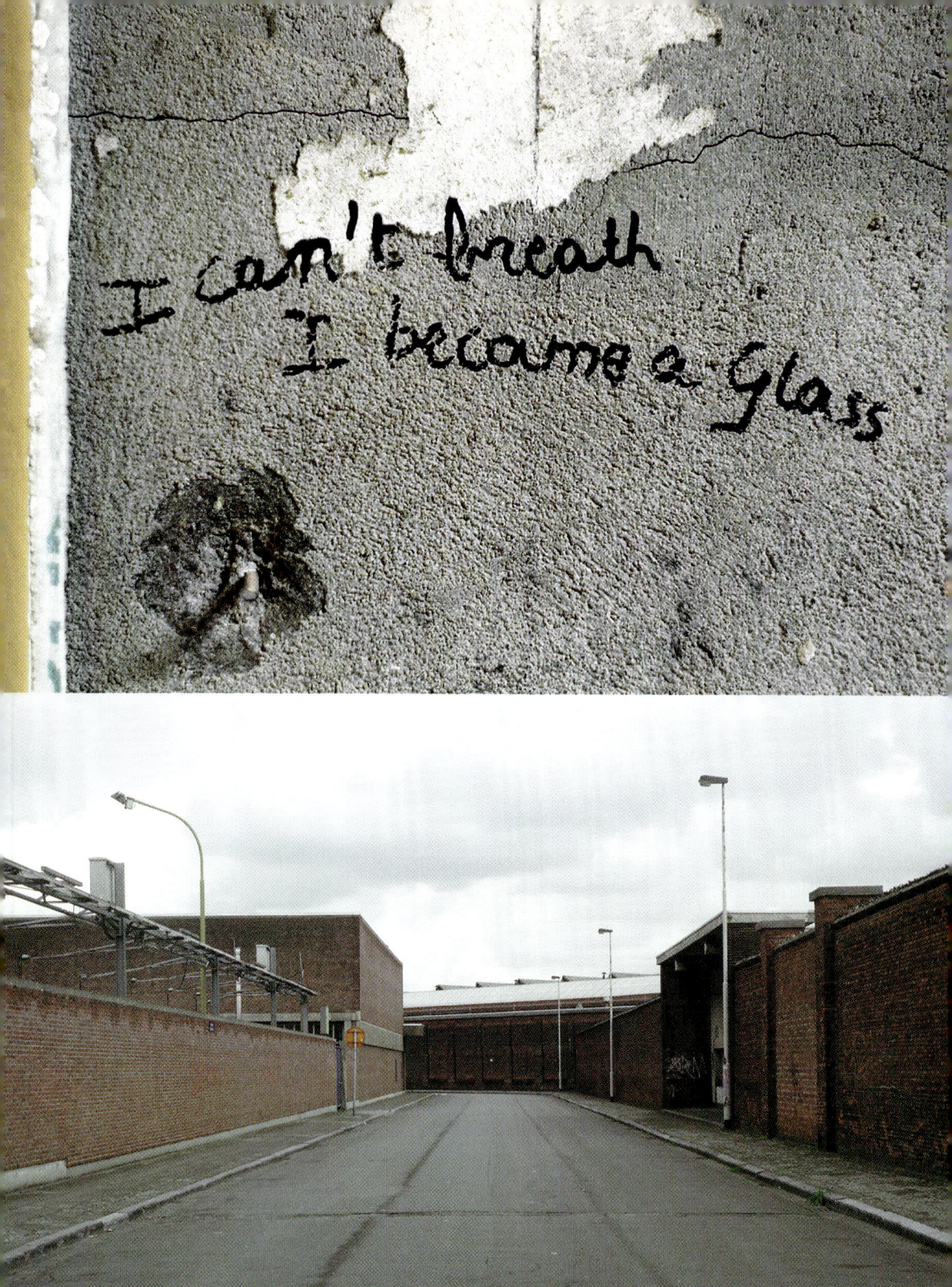

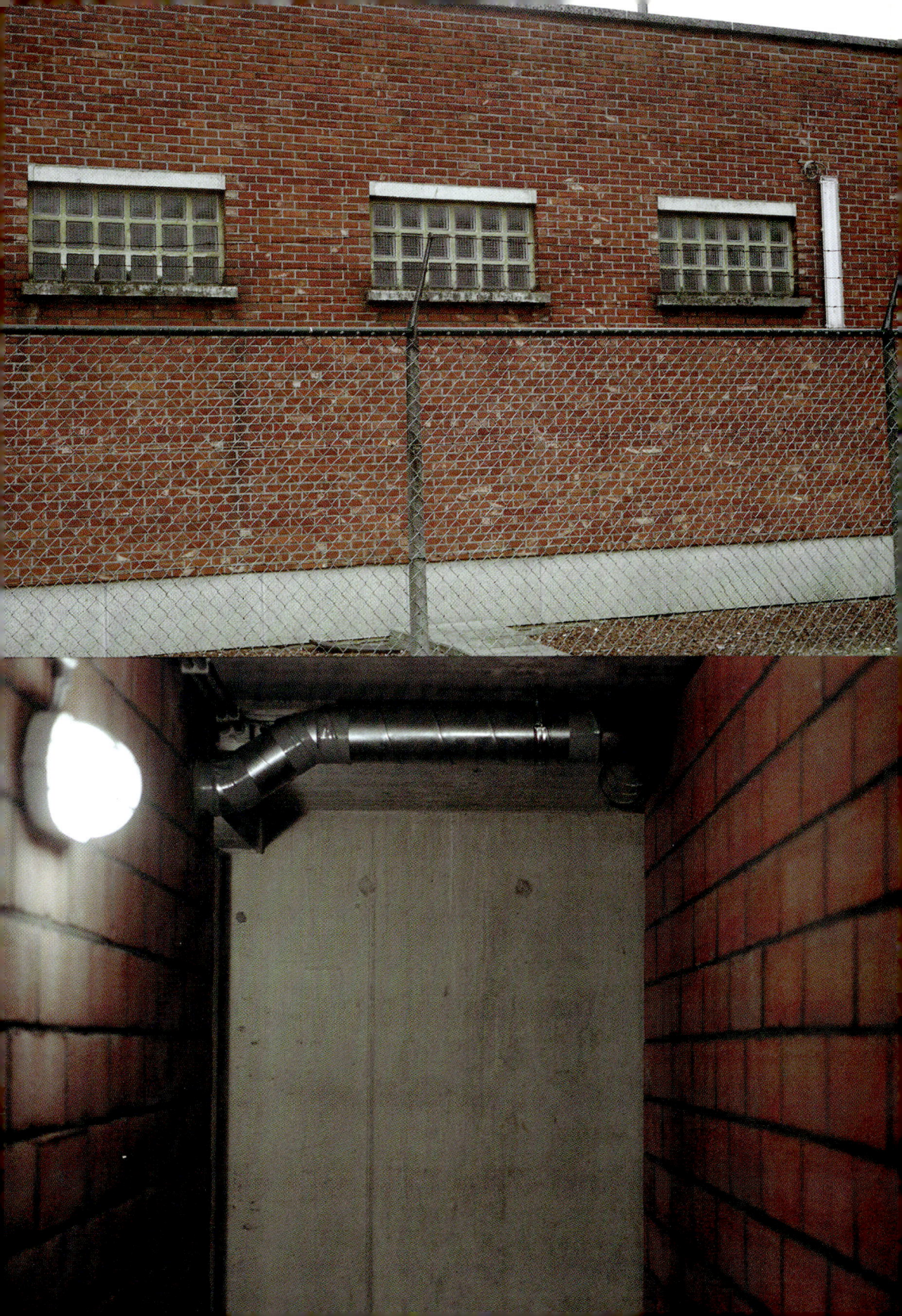

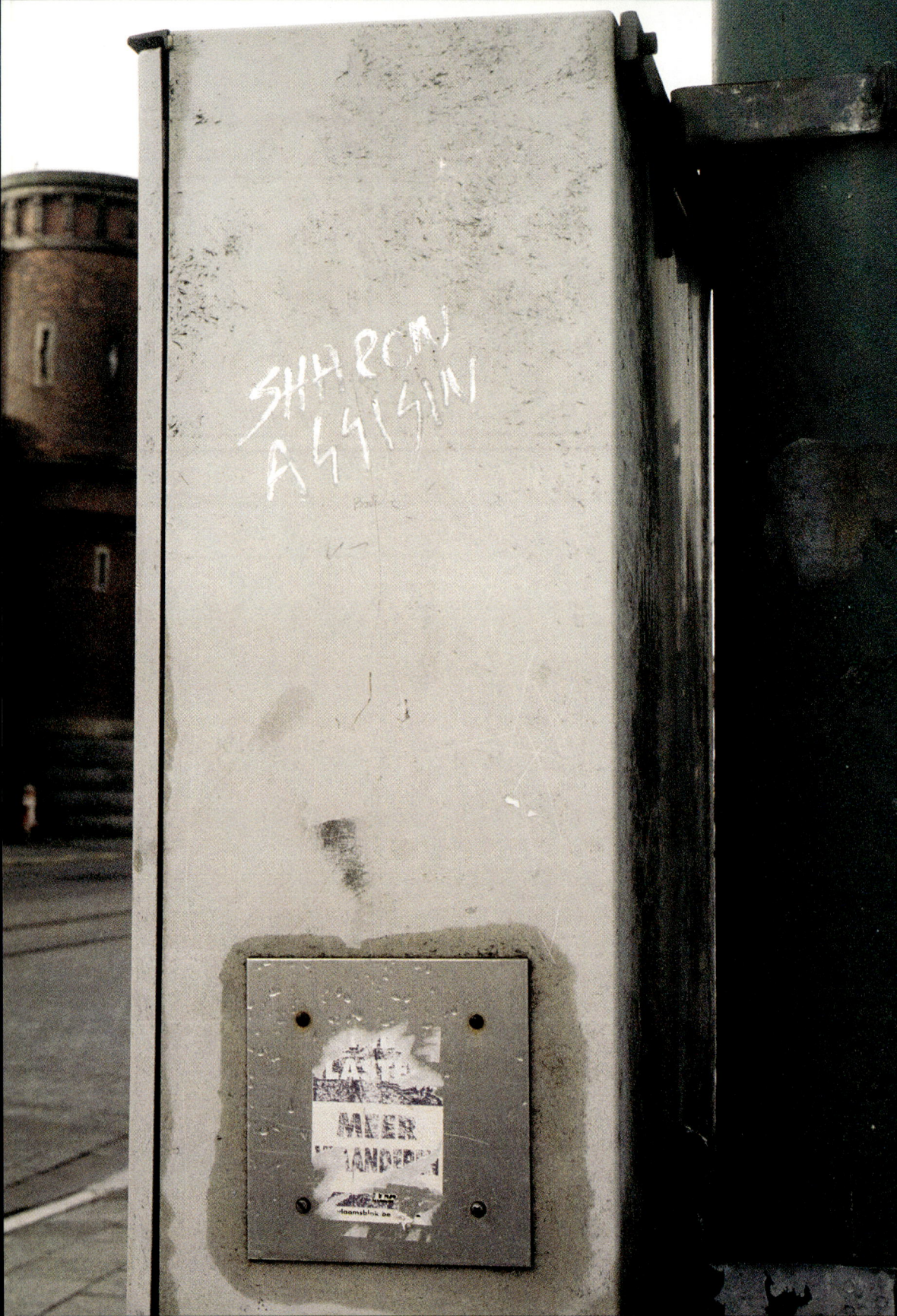

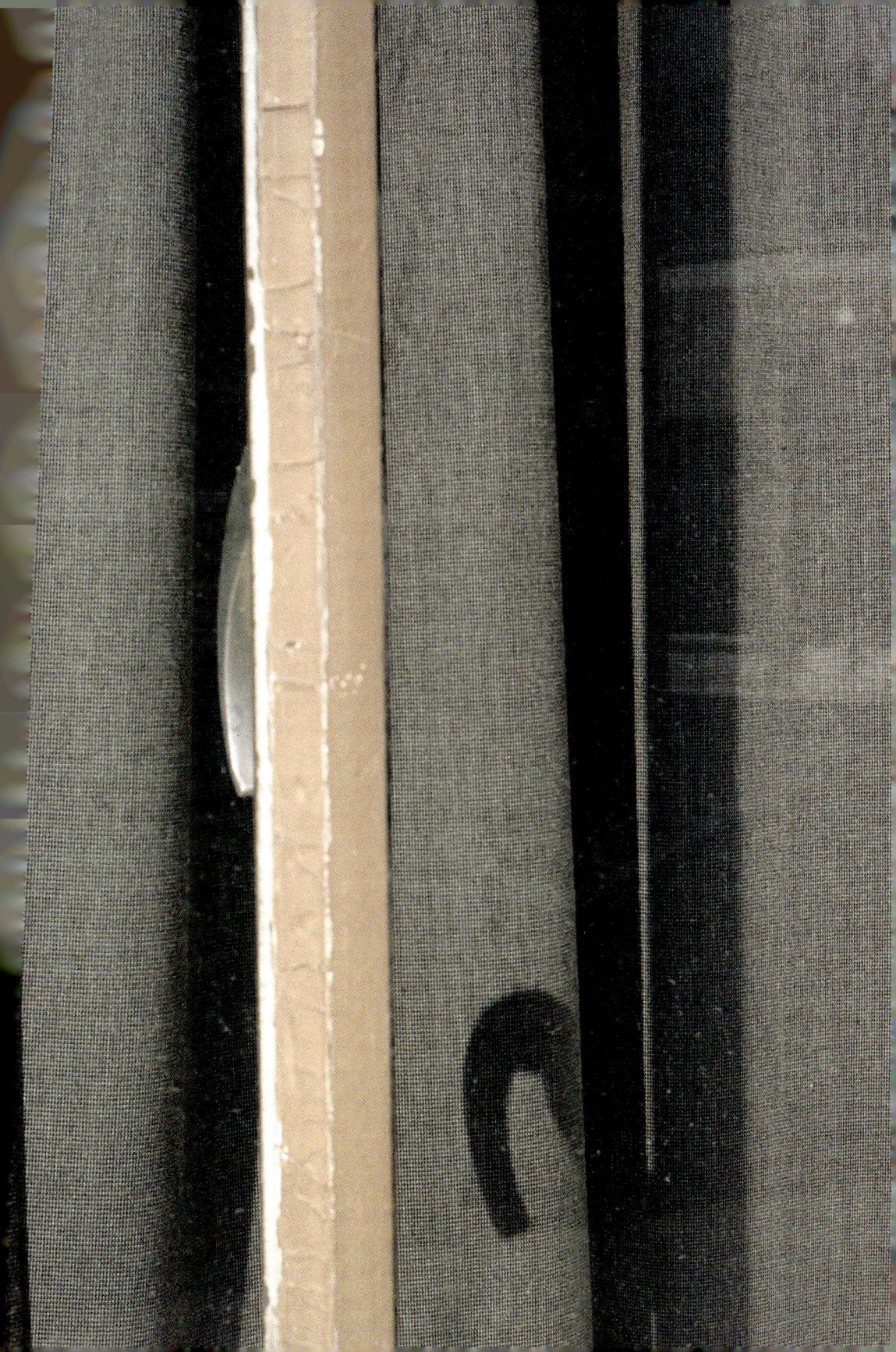

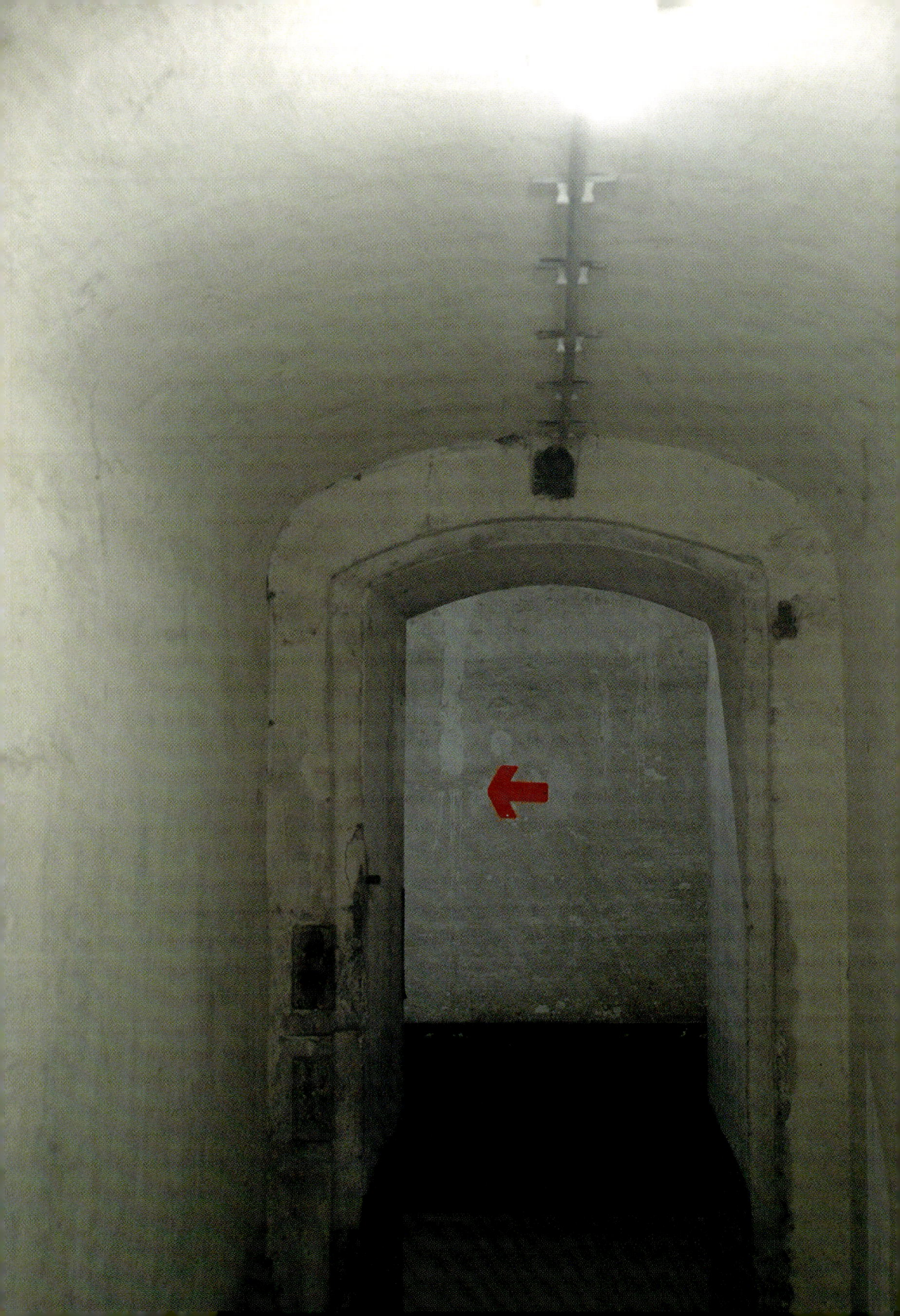

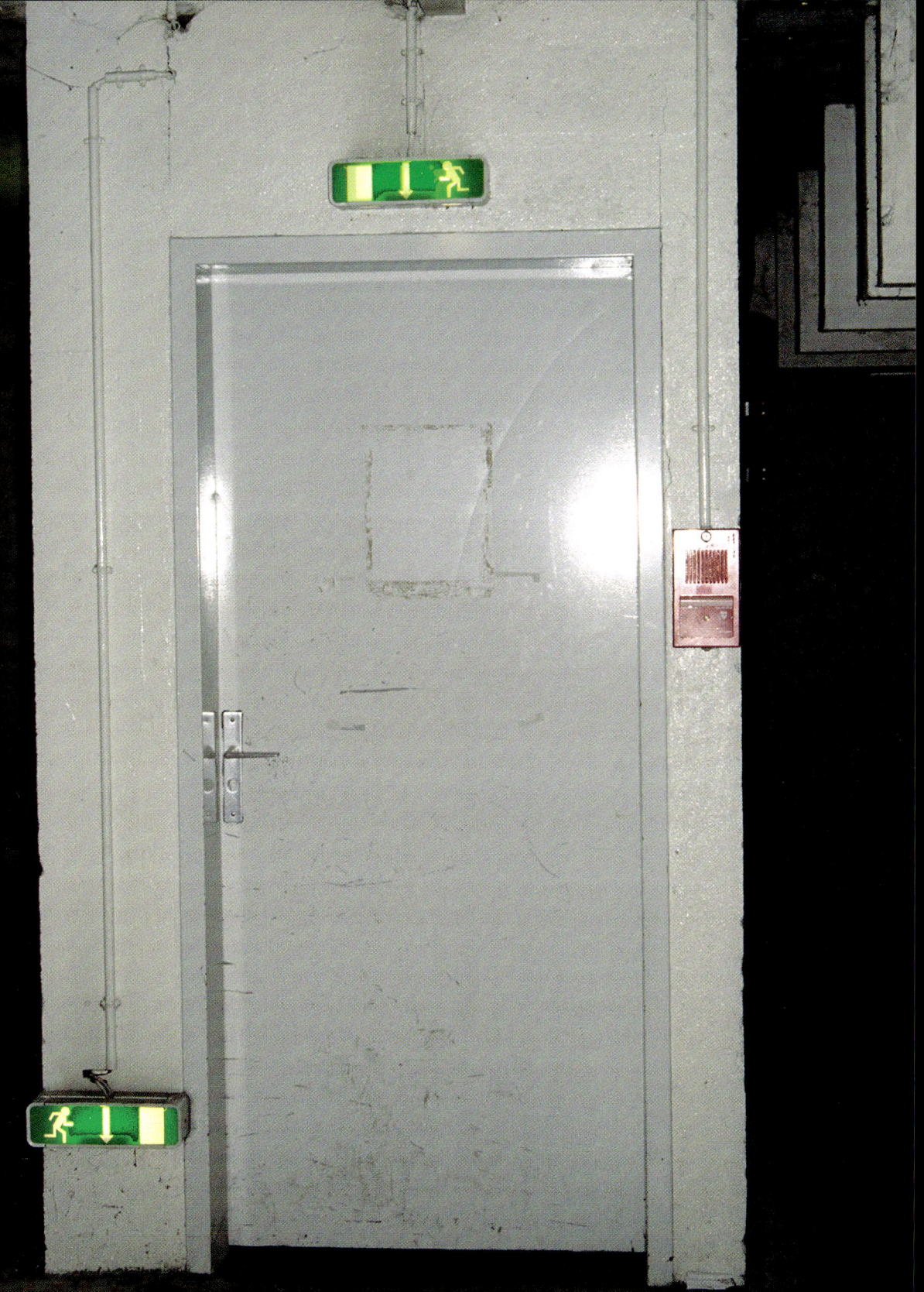

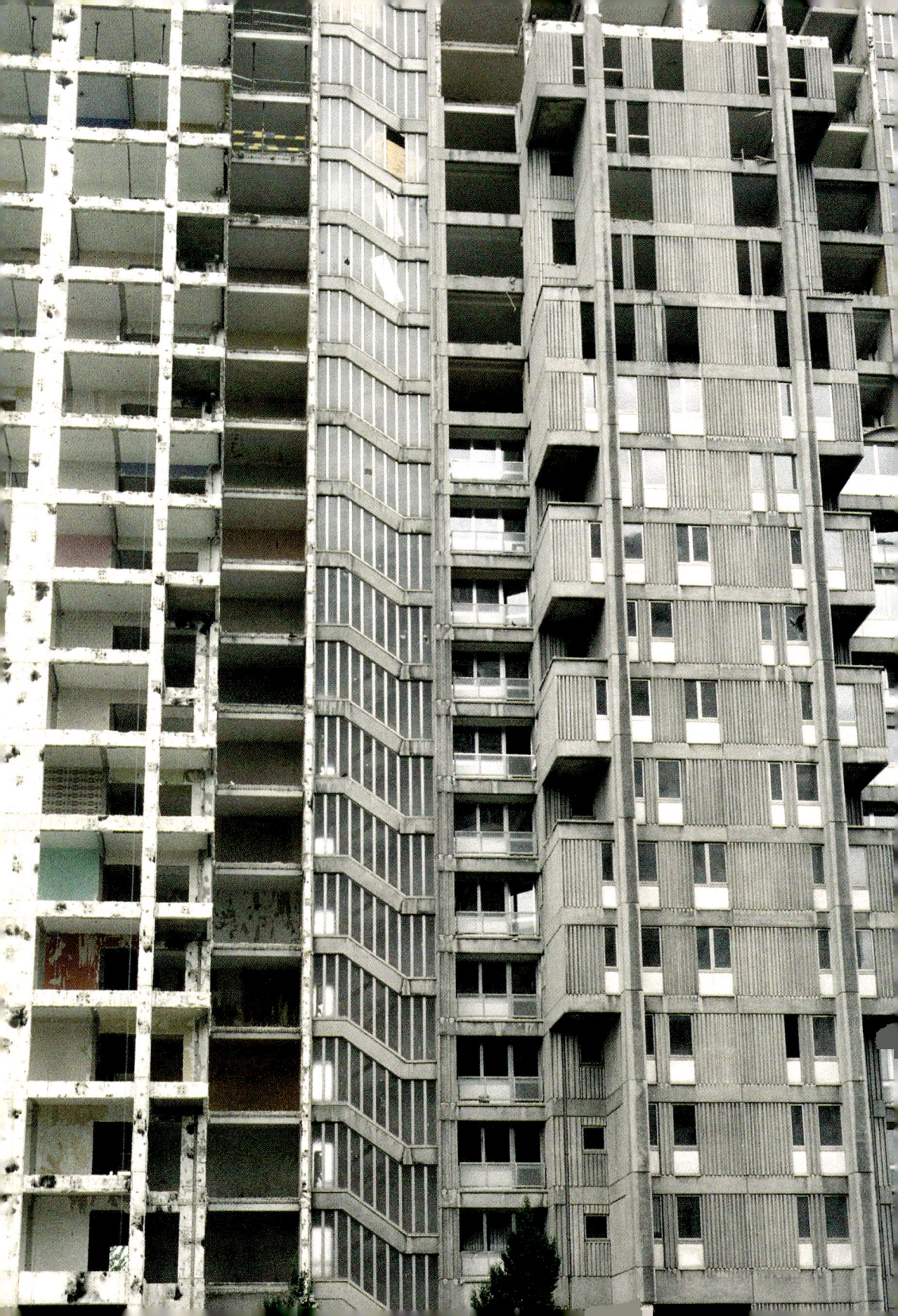

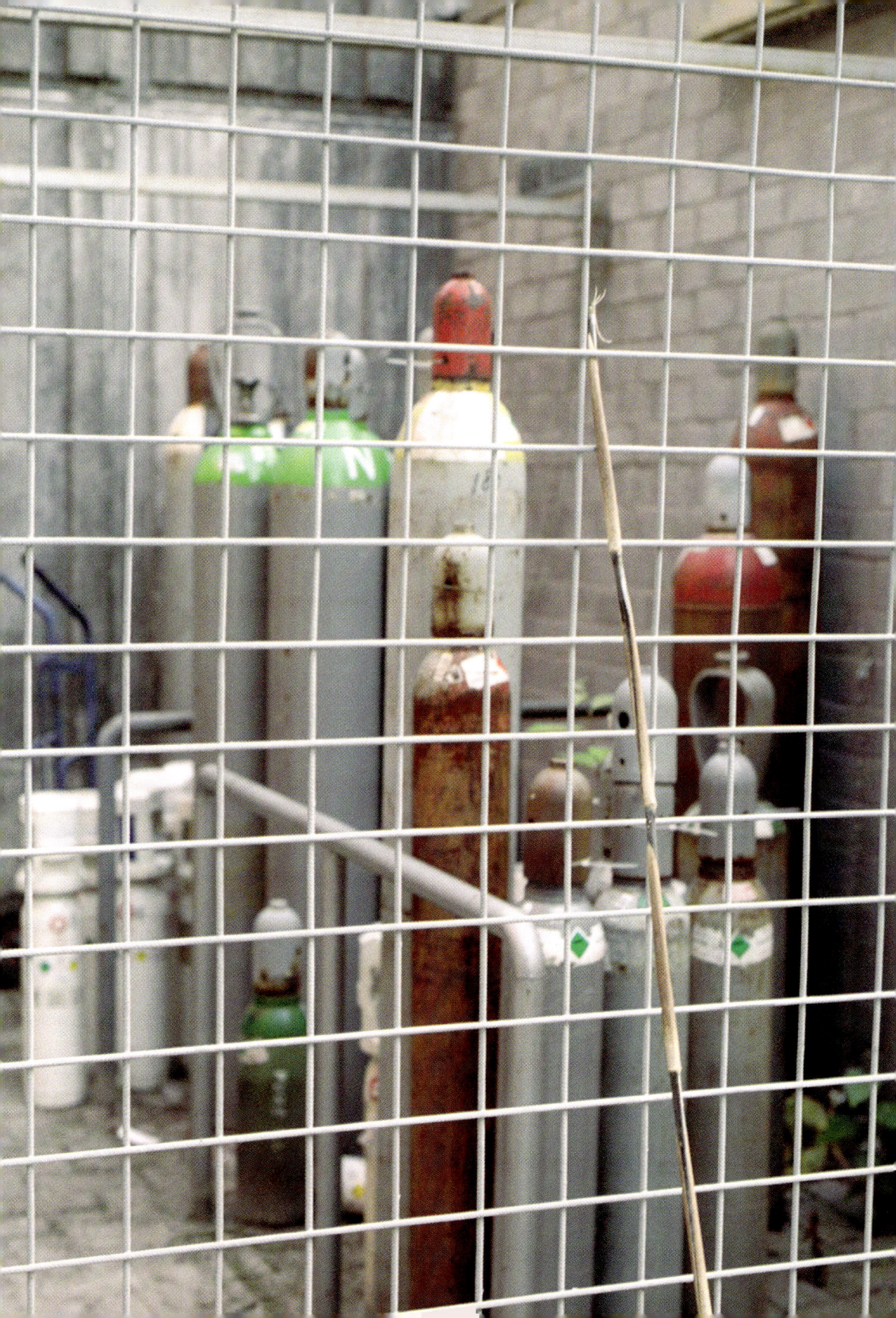

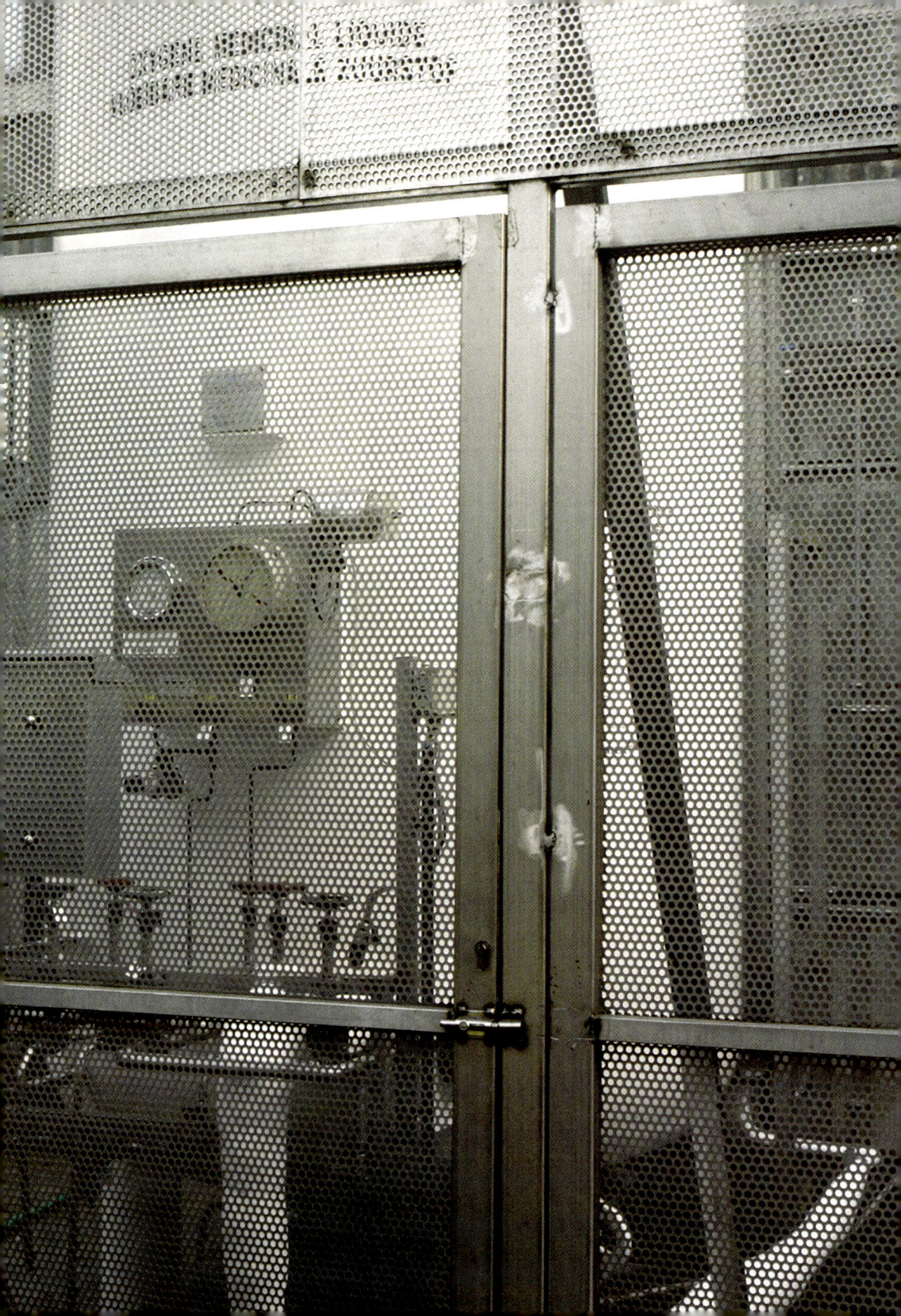

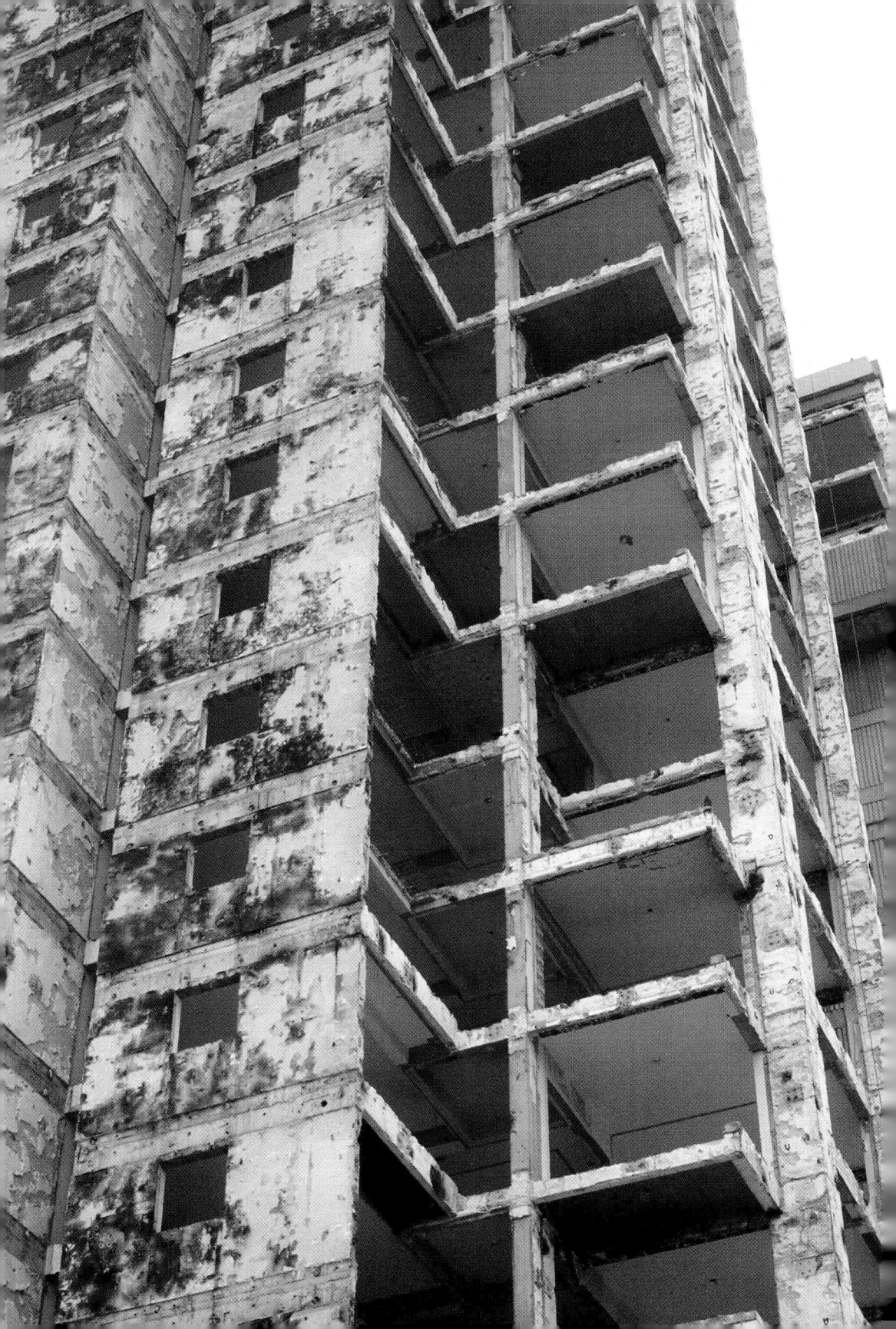

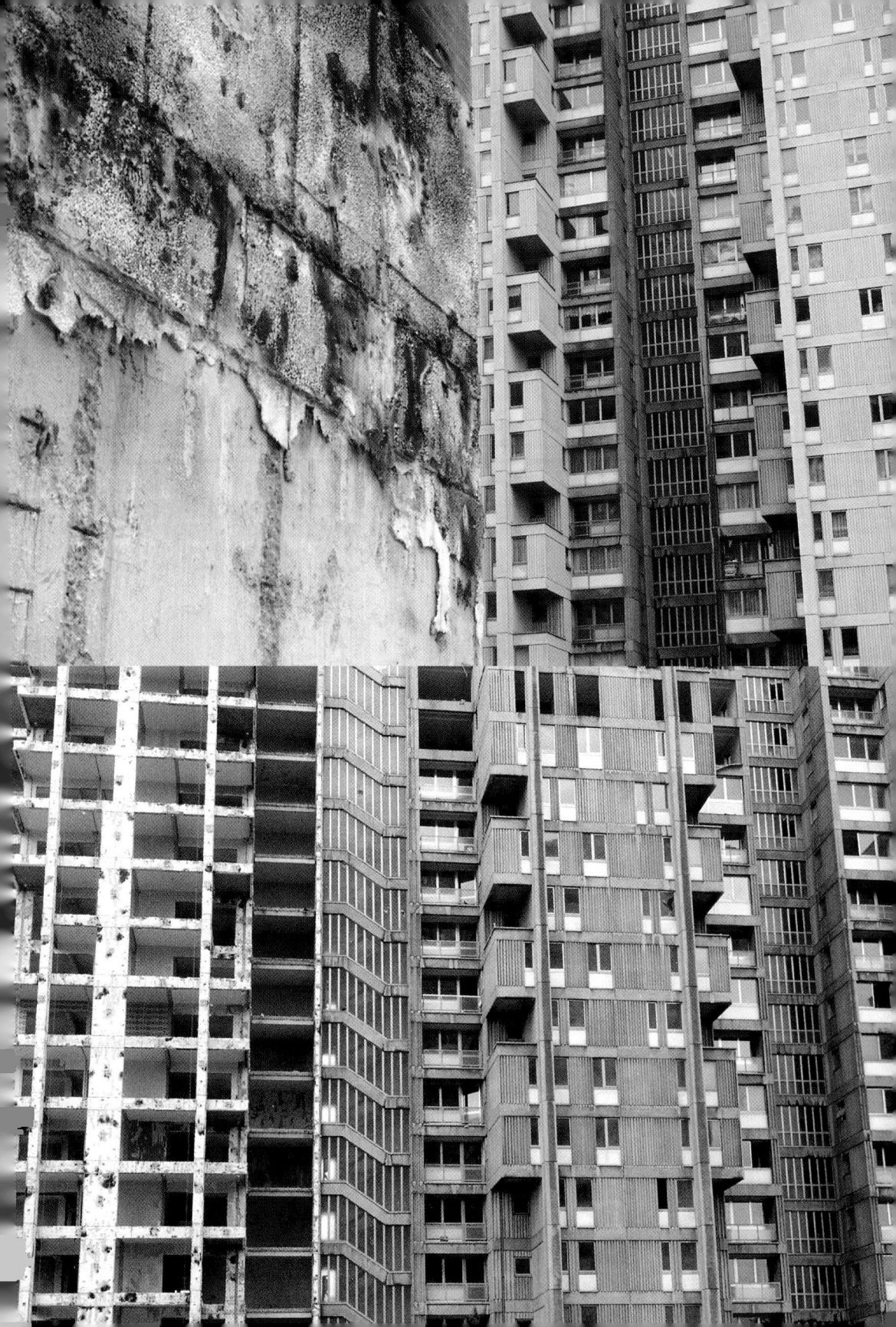

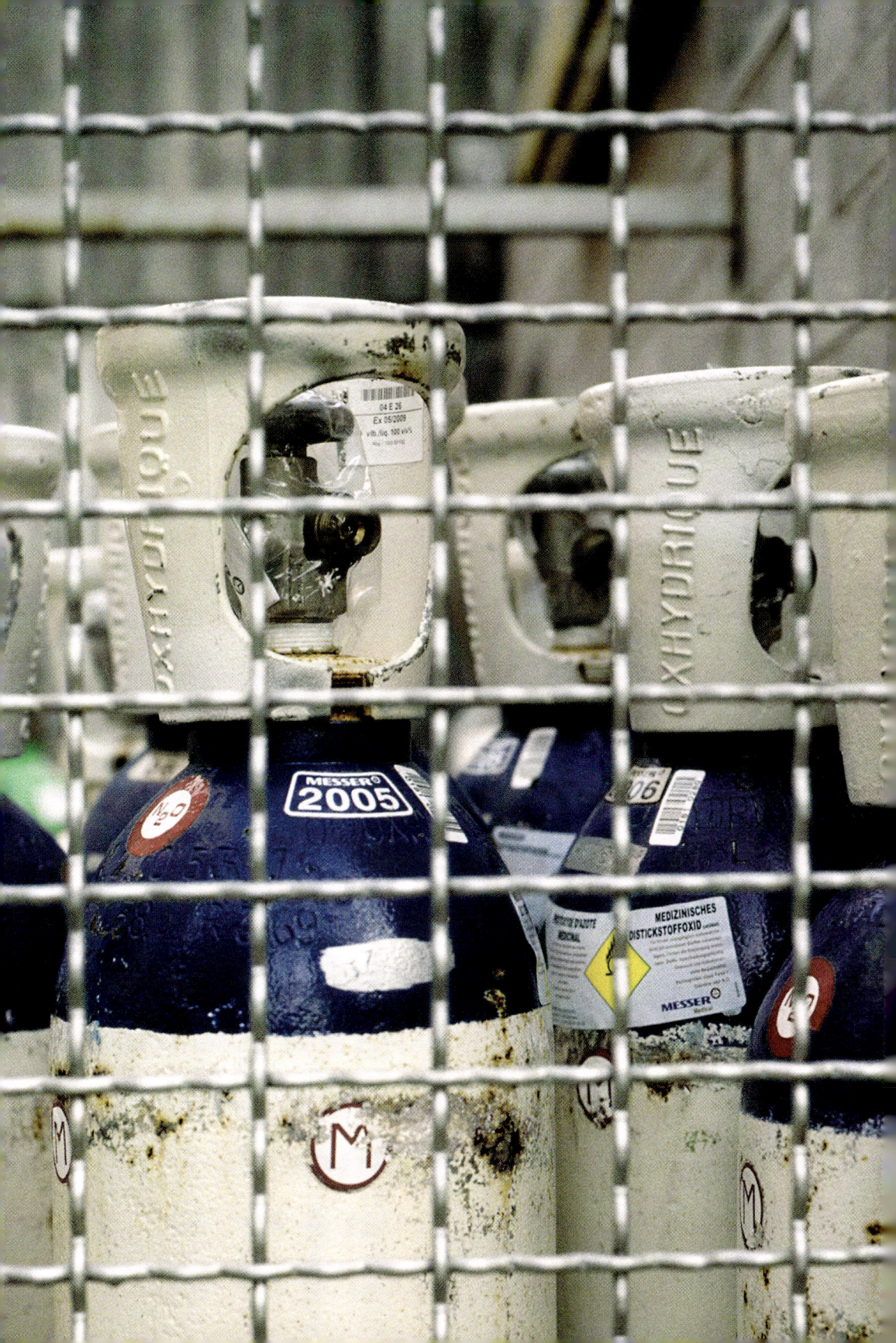

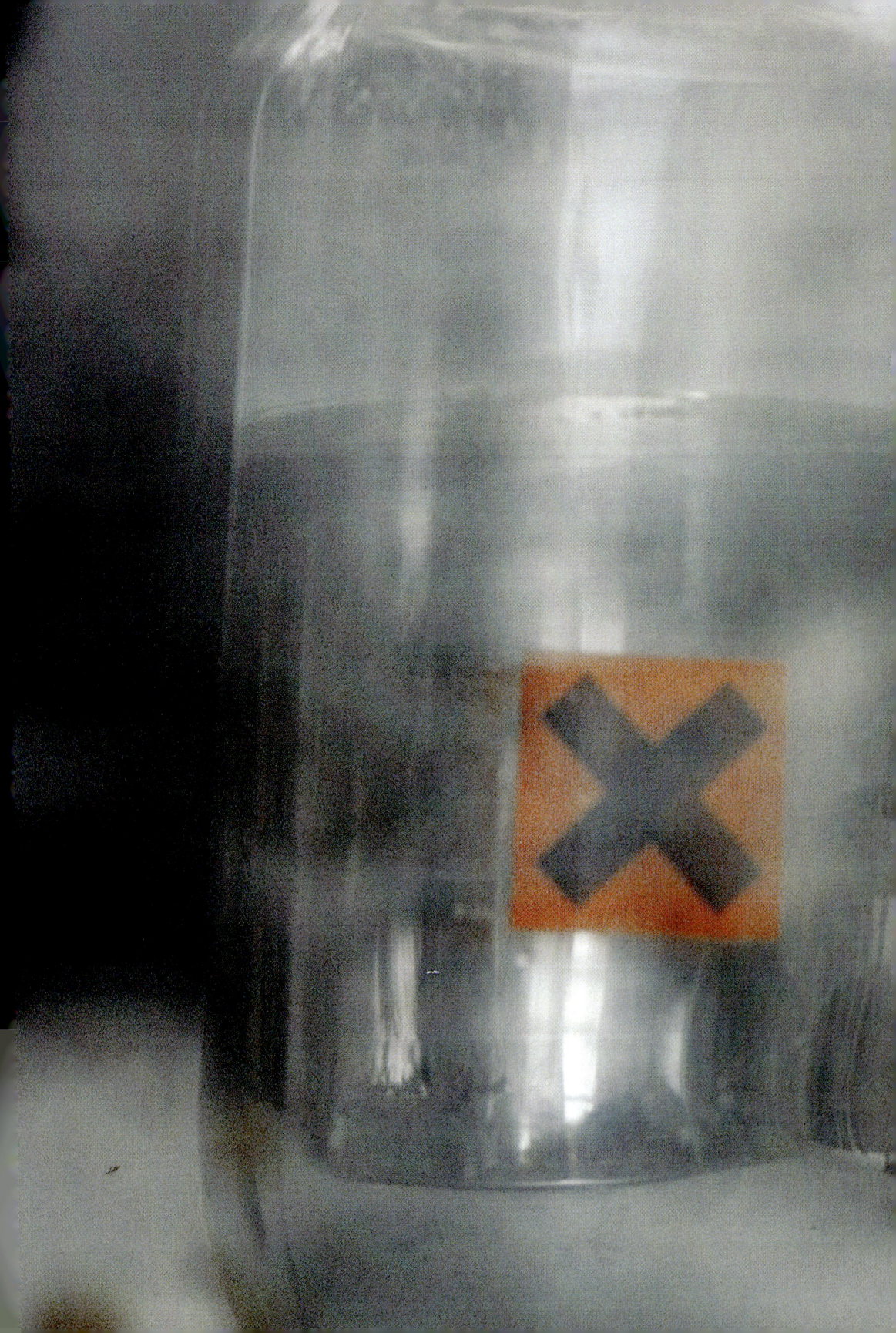

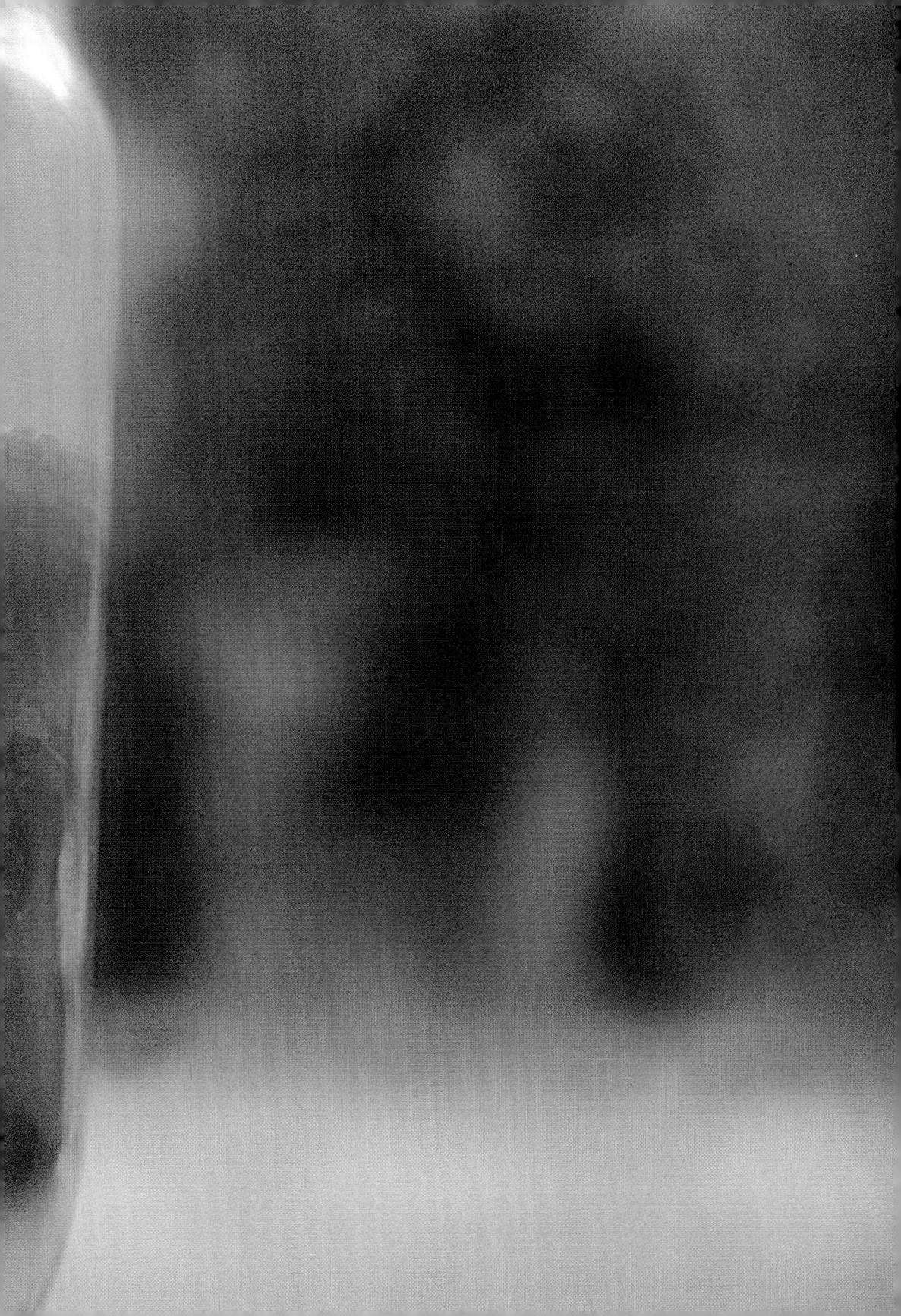

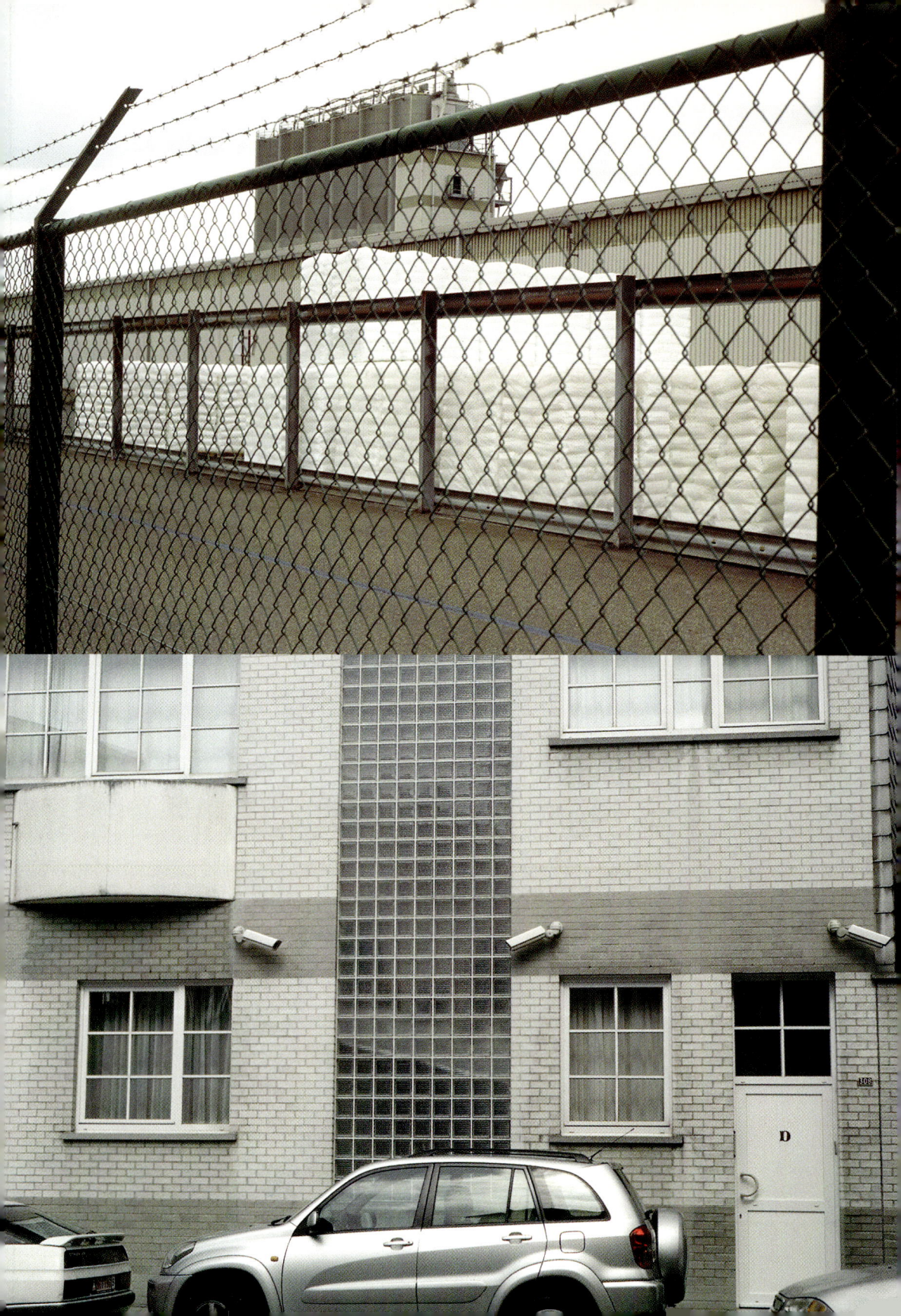

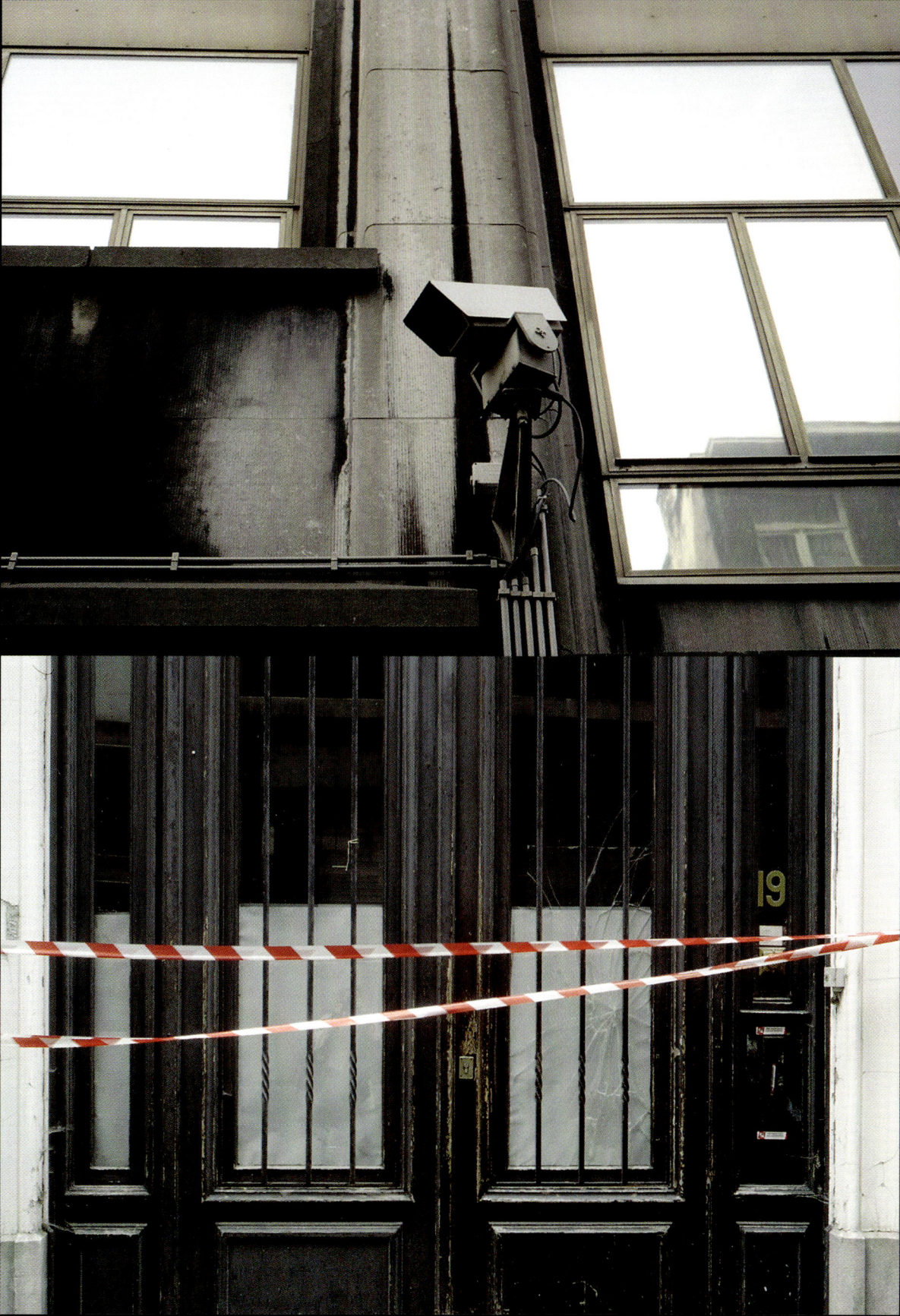

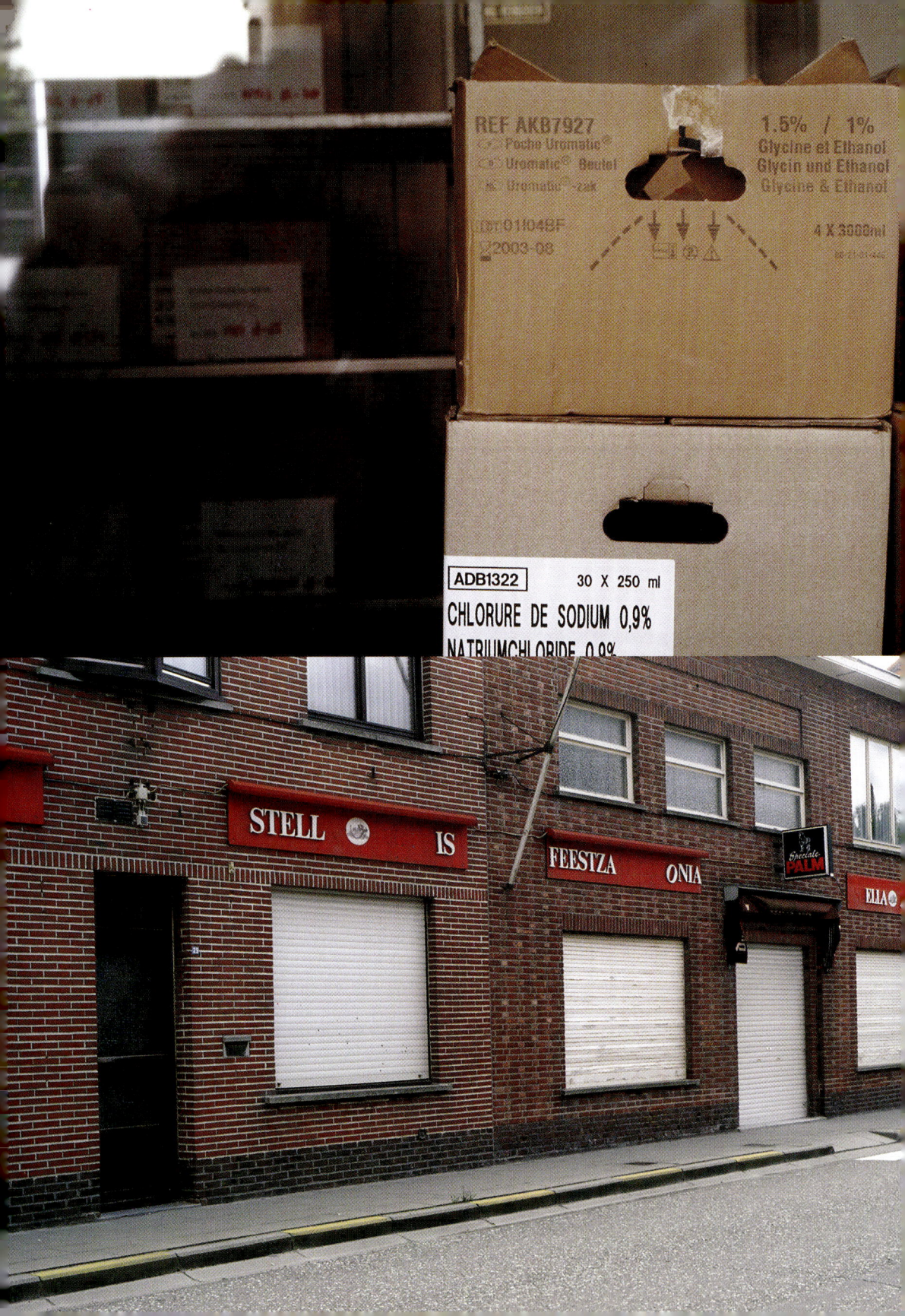

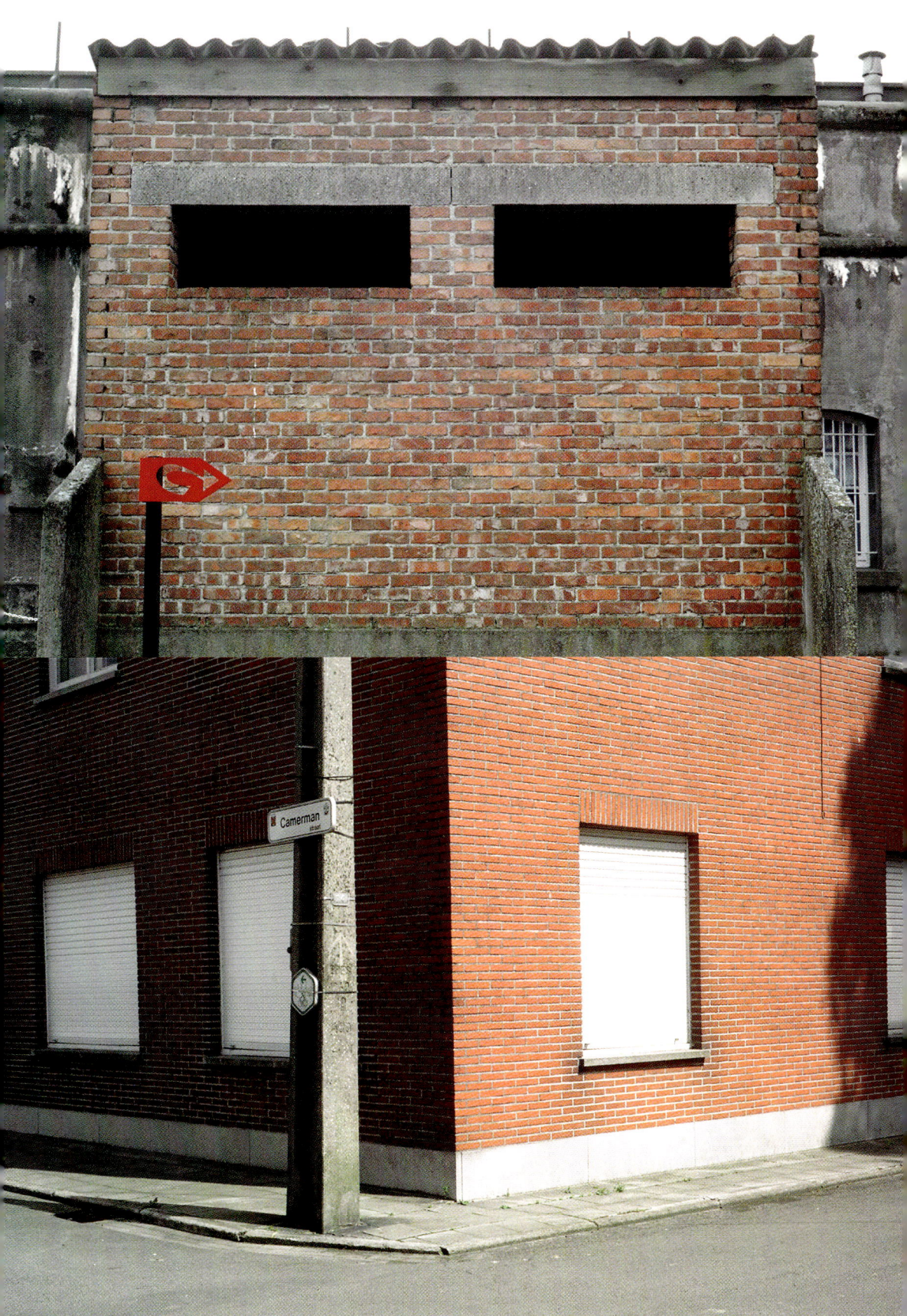

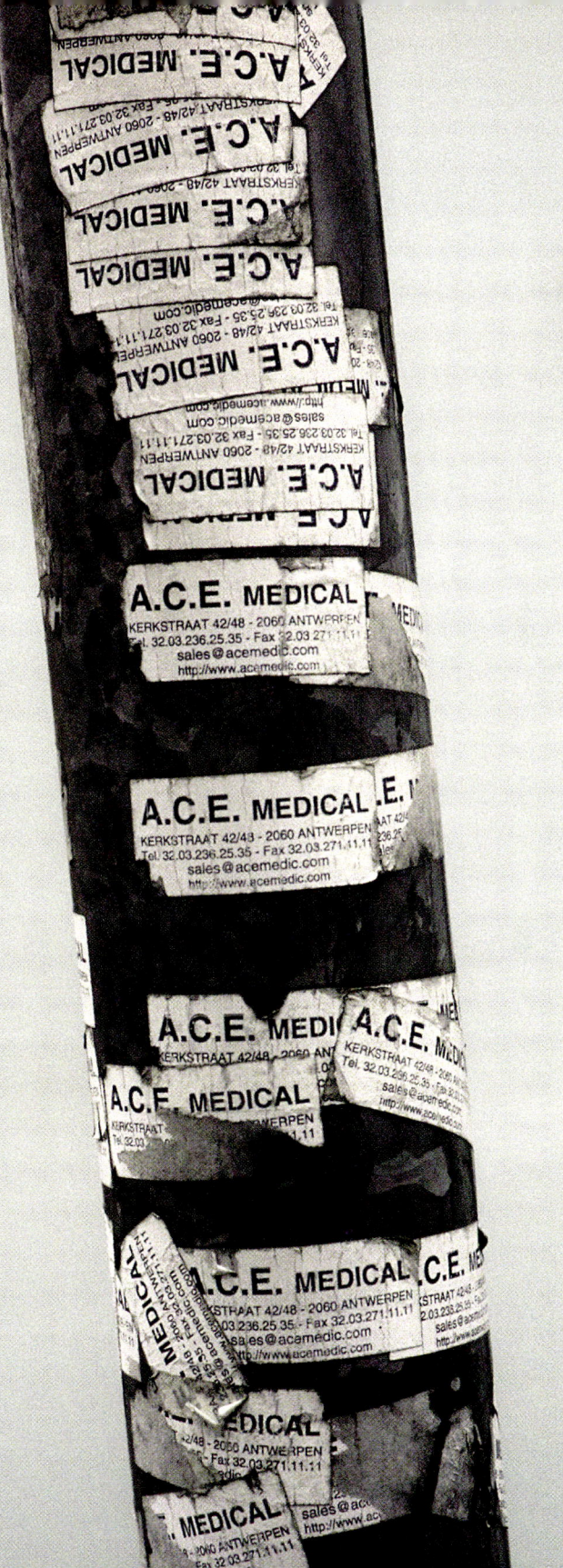

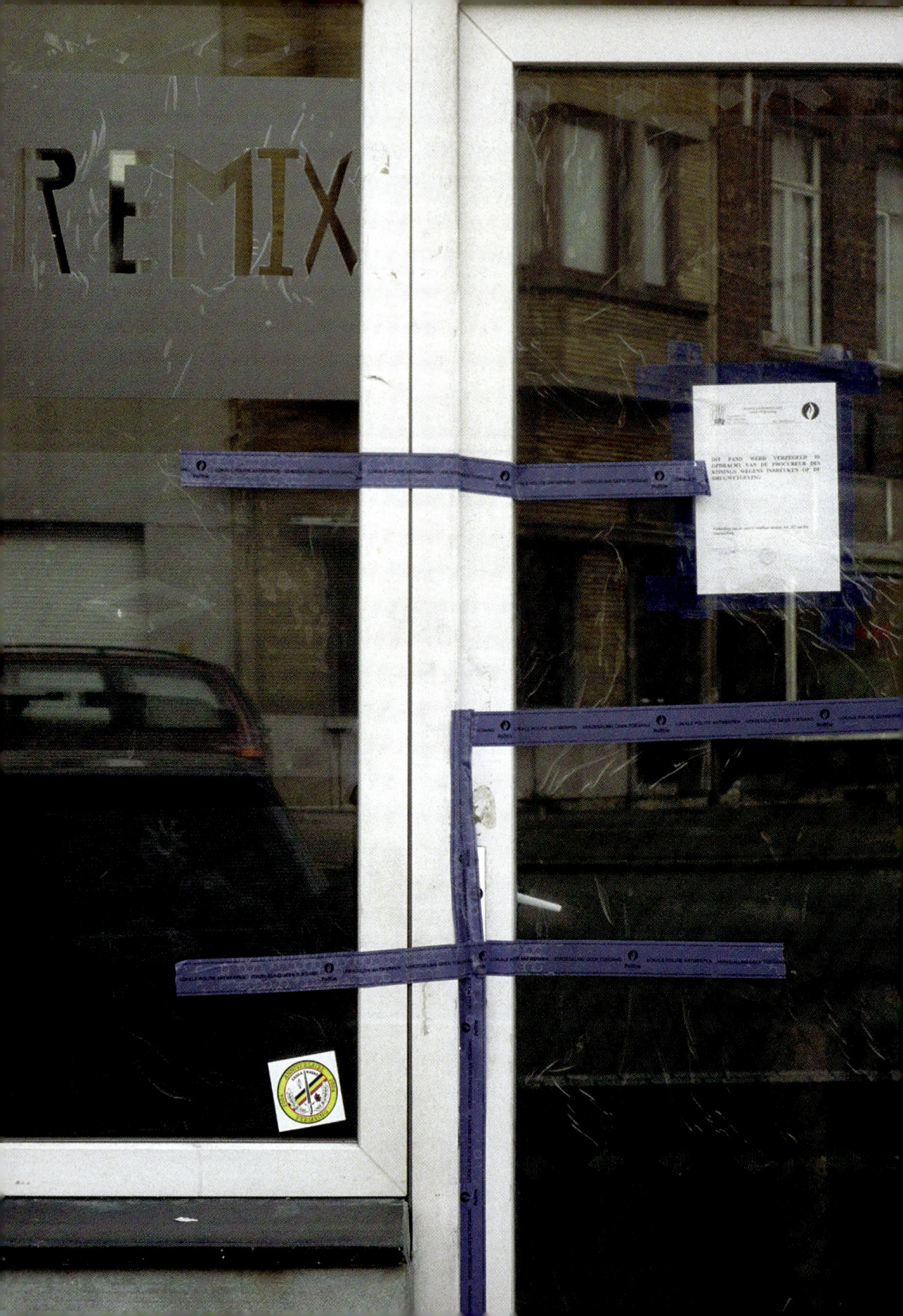

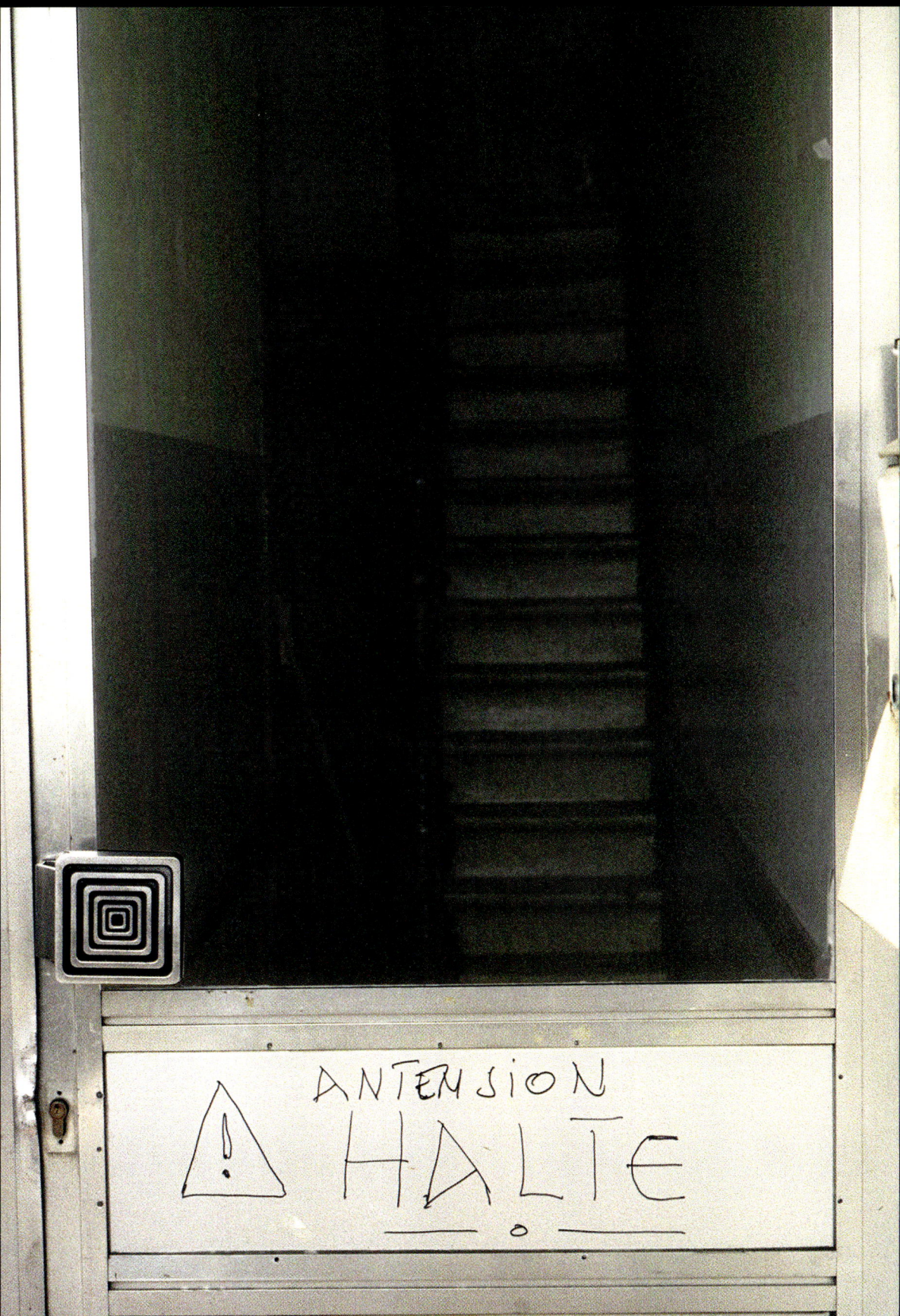

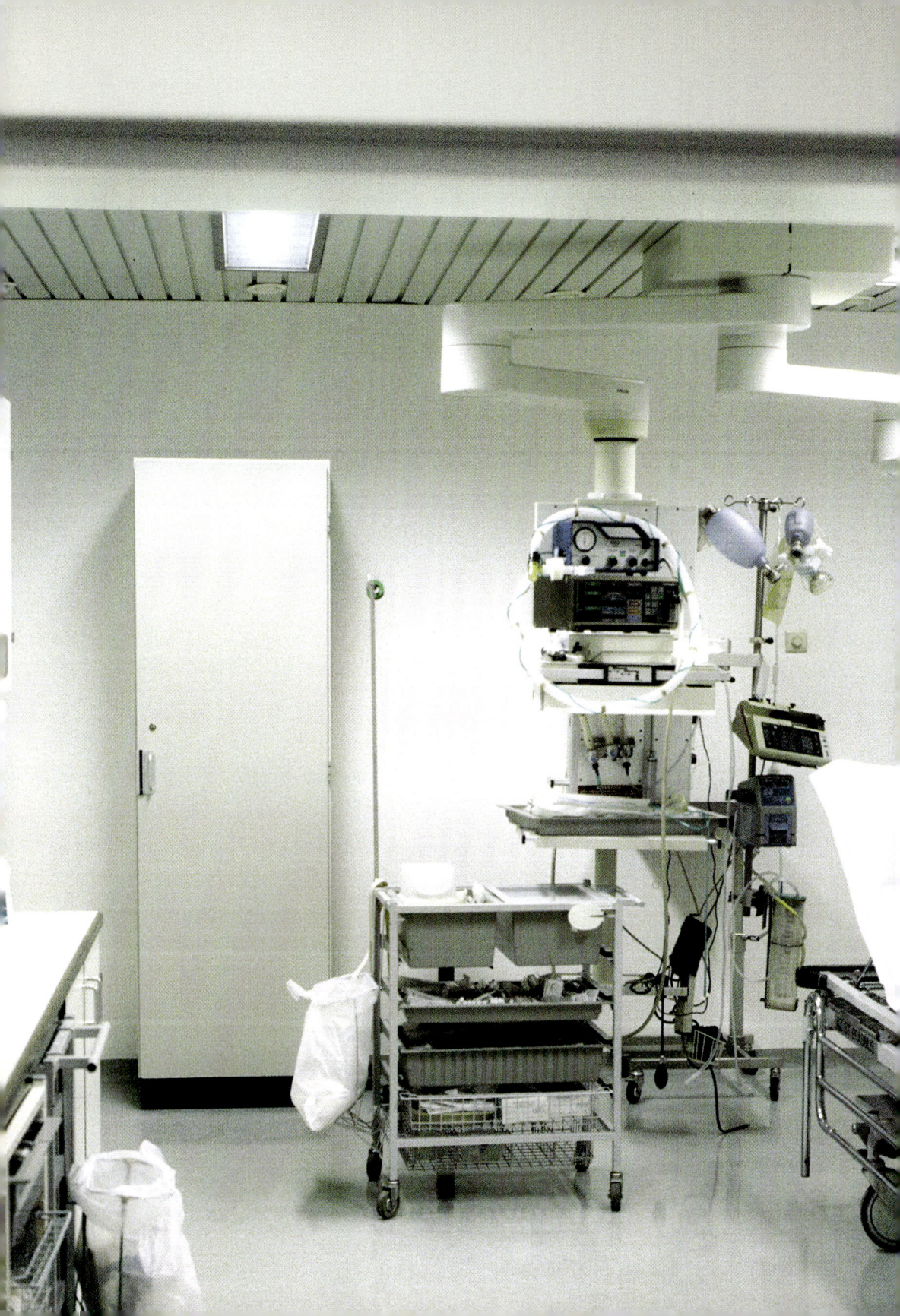

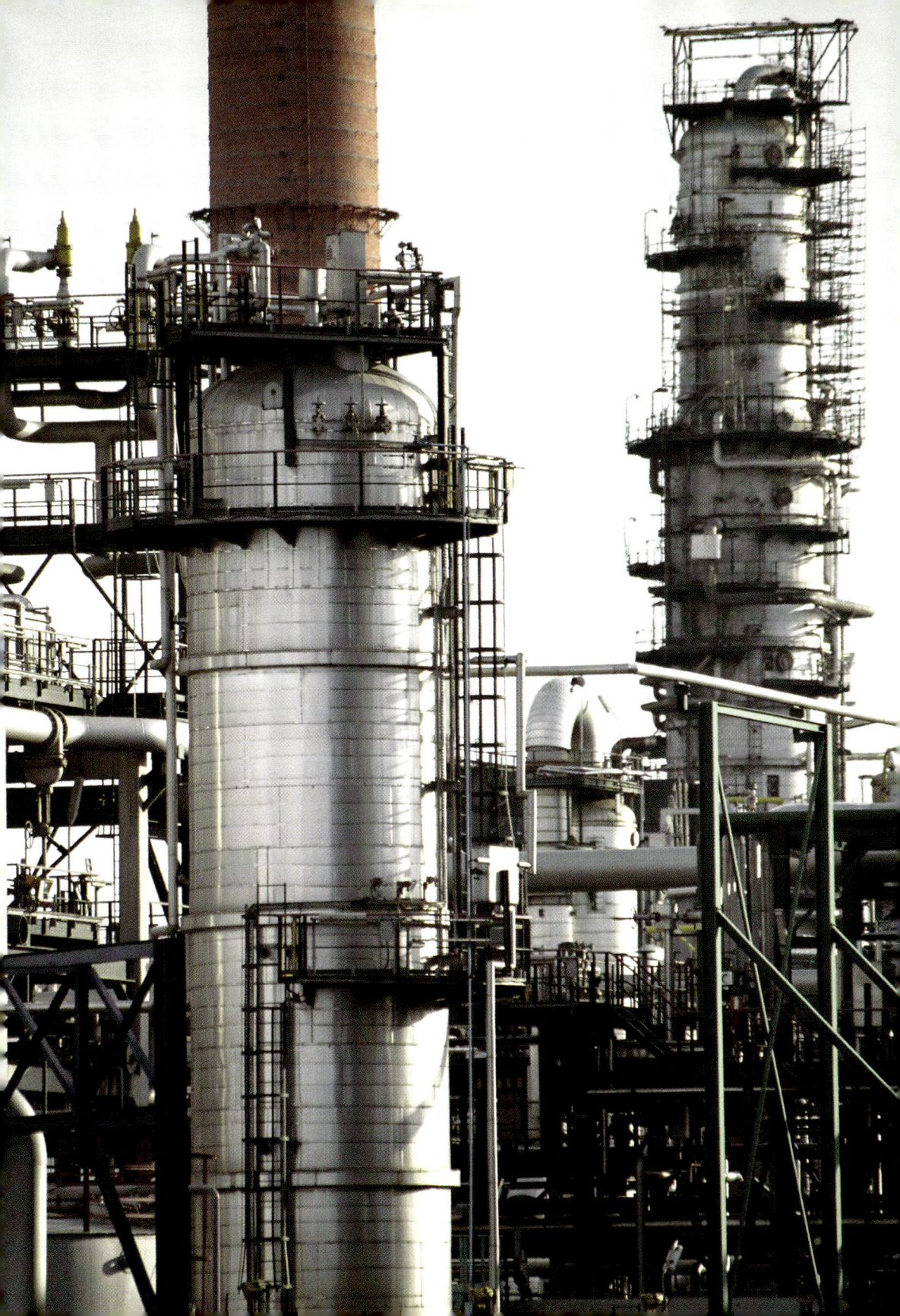

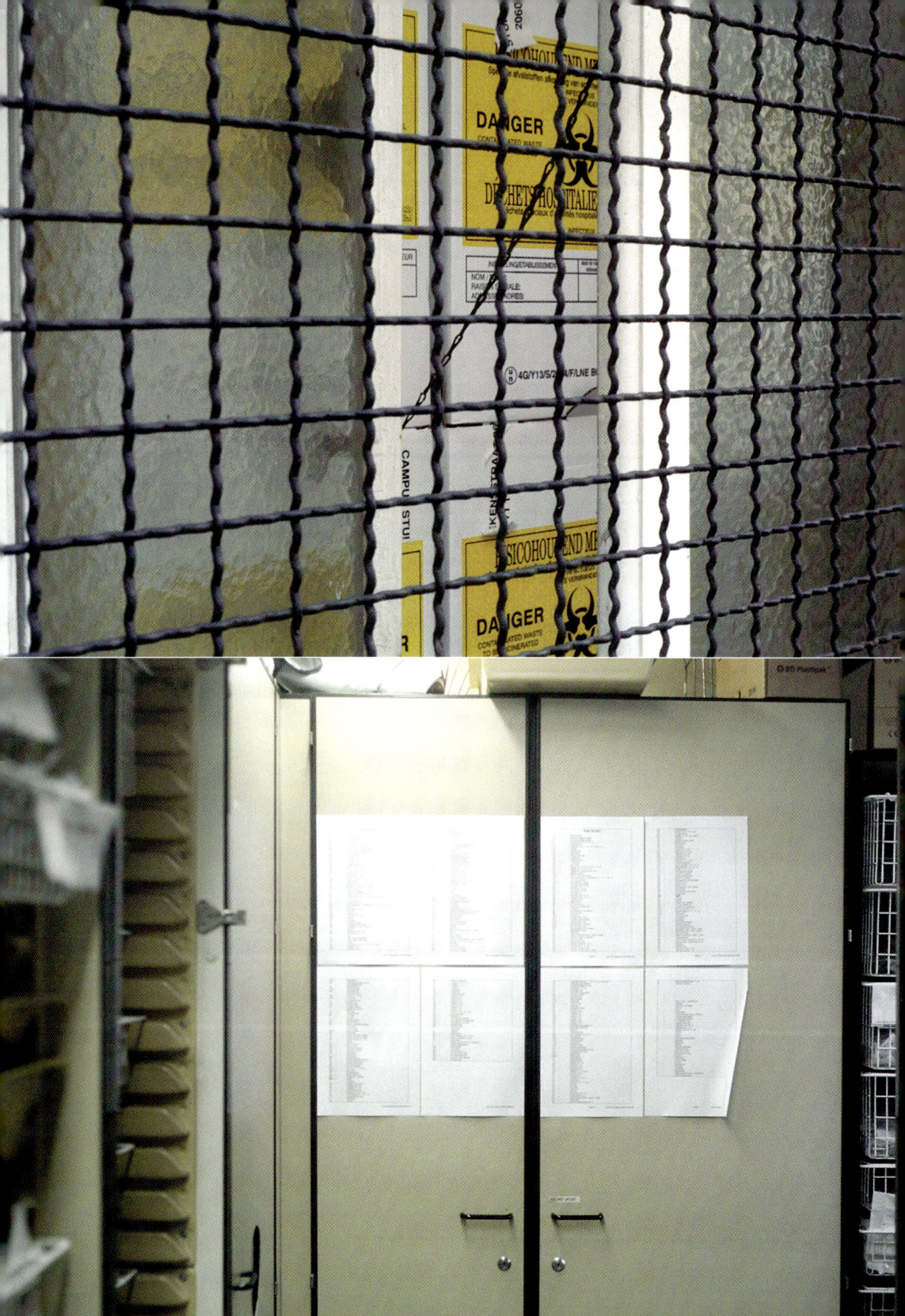

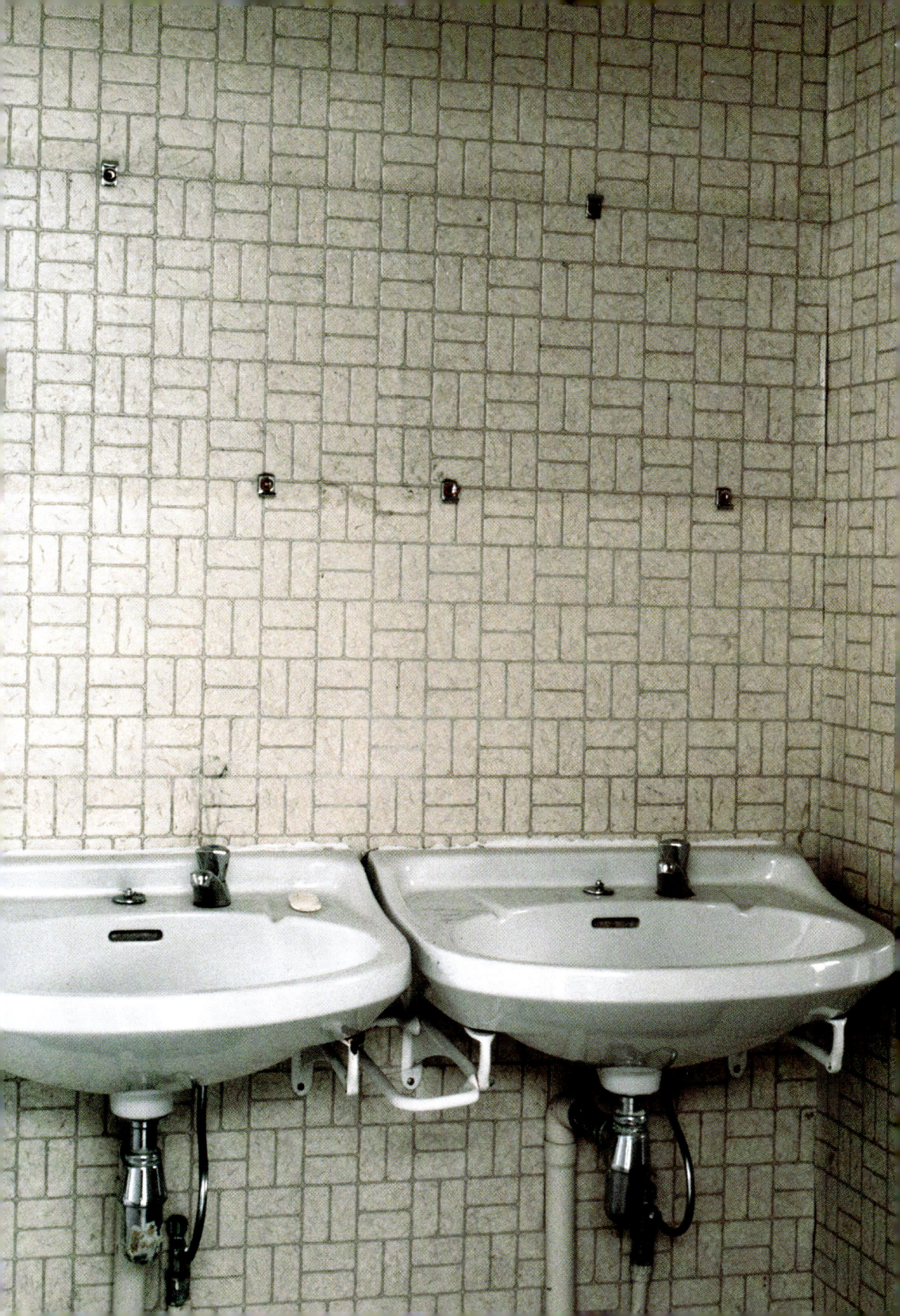

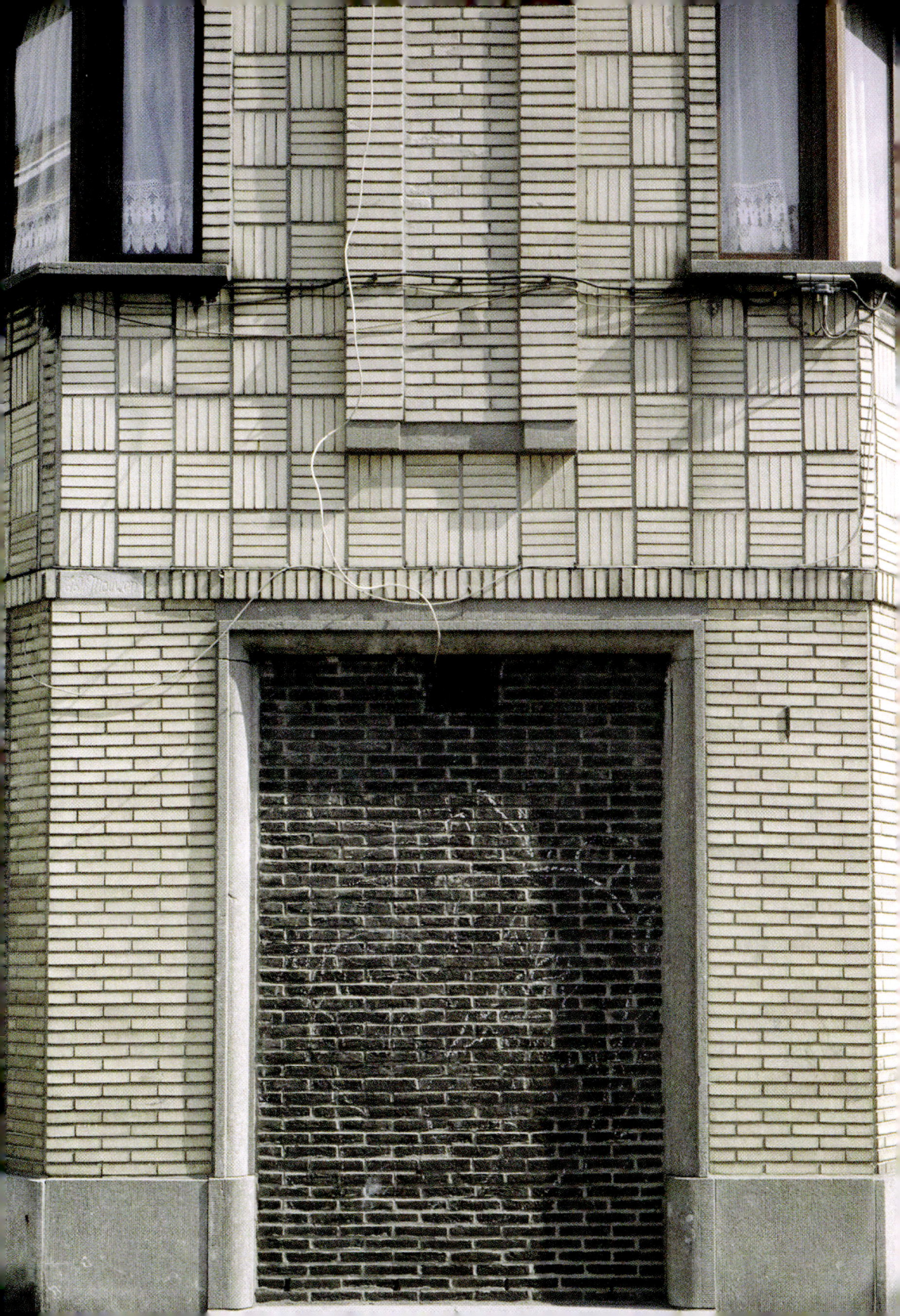

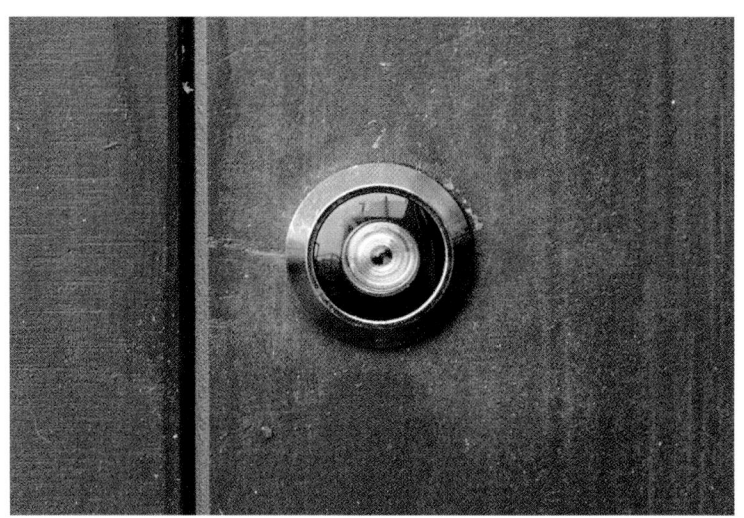

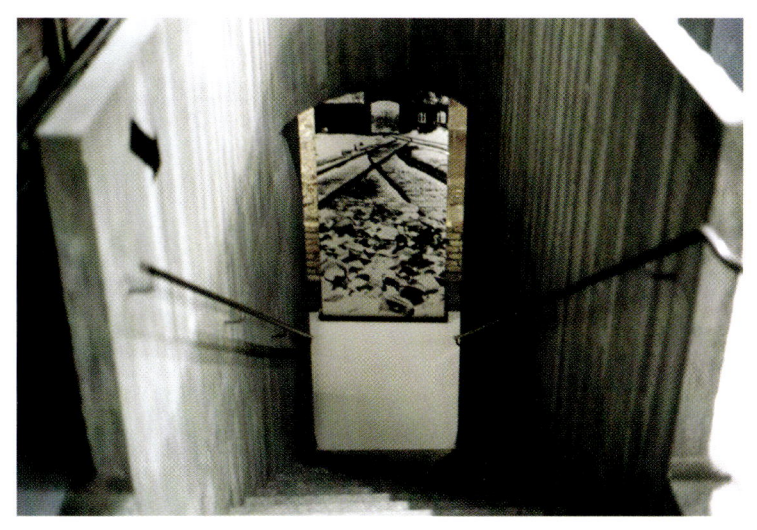

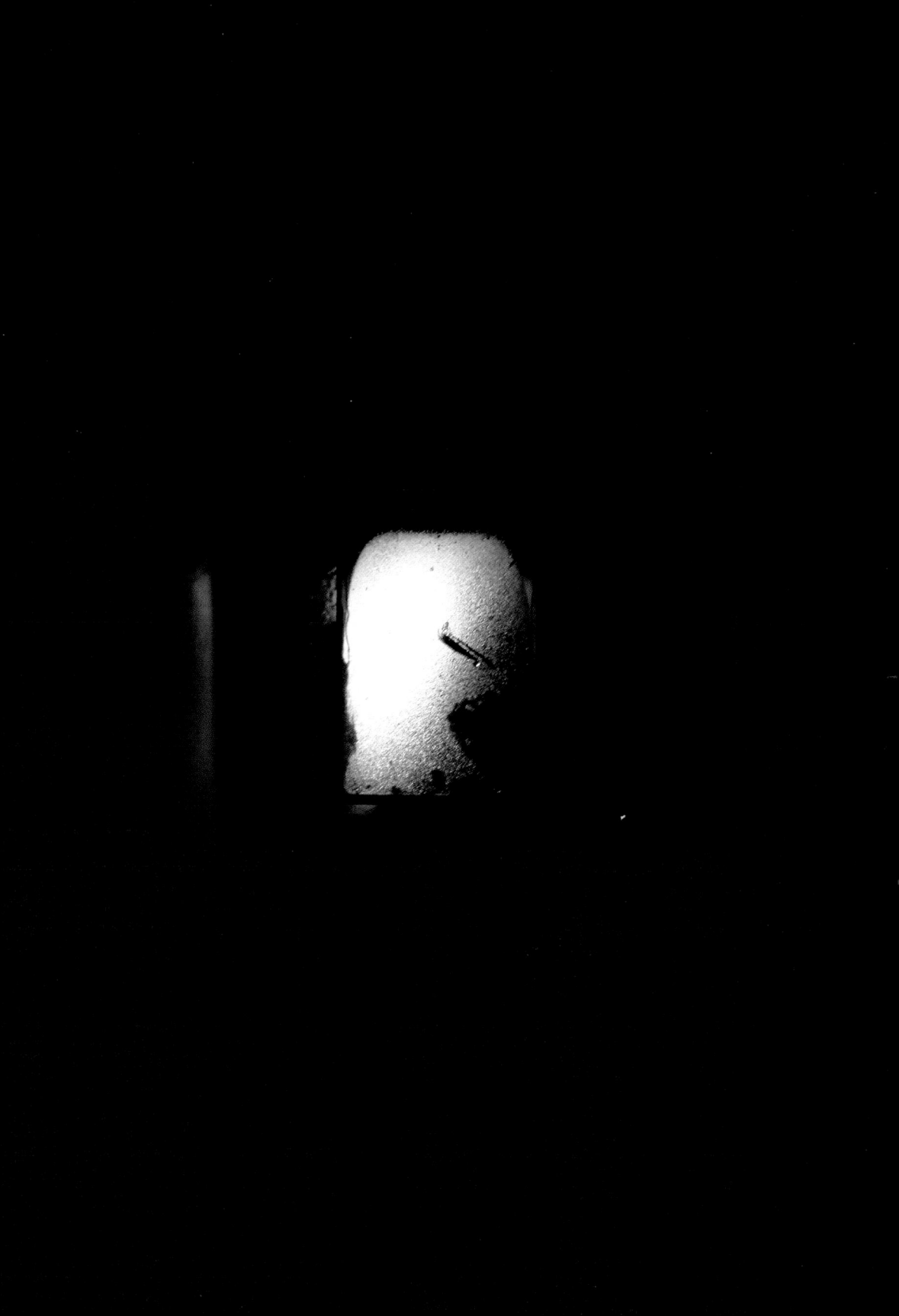

there are certain places...

where inescapable things have happened...

...areas around us

clinging to points in time...

there are interiors and exteriors that breathe

their own prophesies;

places where a combination of events

have merged together

VISITATION into a fusion of actualities...

there are places where air

matter and perception have collided

along the strand of equilibriums,

spilling universes into the floorboards,

casting novae across the ceilings...

corridors along the way

blare the cicatrix of these moments

like mute sirens.

walls and windows are forever

reciting to us what they have witnessed,

whispering their tales

in short distilled sentences,

reverberating the echo of absent hours

so explicitly

they make no sound…

my senses crawl

in between the paint and plaster,

feeling for the nanosecond,

that lingering sigh

trapped beneath the pavement.

my eyes scan the gases

holding the day together.

swimming this translucent volume,

I separate the carbon from the monoxide,

excavating the inertia

between my body and the bricks,

sailing the unobtrusive moons

between now and then.

for somewhere

in one of these places

there is a particular instant

awaiting me.

somewhere, at this very moment,

there is a proverbial Mercury,

transiting dark orbits,

carrying a combination of events

within his hold...

each path brings me closer

towards this impact

of atmosphere and anatomy.

when all the surfaces surrounding me

shall mirror my angst.

I wonder what colour the sky will be

on the day that we meet?

I wonder what shade of light

will fill that inevitable room?

when you suddenly appear from around the corner,

upon the hour are we to converge

and rattle,

what exotic fuels will you burn,

as we engage,

pitching sinister logarithms into the air...

bending the afternoon backwards...

turning space inside-out...

winding amnesia around the silence...

Alice Evermore 2004

Els Vanden Meersch studied visual arts at the Sint-Lukas Hogeschool Brussels, was a post-graduate of the Higher Institute of Visual Arts, Antwerp, and she was a participant at the Rijksakademie voor Beeldende Kunst, Amsterdam. Her work consists of (site specific) installations and photography, in which she explores the psychological structures of architecture and how this defines the position of the individual and its self image. In 2003 she published her first photo book Transient constructions, a selection of her photo archive from 1996-2003 (Antwerp, Landschap & Portret vzw, Genk Flac©, 2003).

Hilde Van Gelder is professor of modern and contemporary art at the KULeuven and, together with Jan Baetens, director of the Lieven Gevaert Research Centre for Photography and Visual Studies at the KULeuven. The author of Hortus panoramicus (Bruges: Stichting Kunstboek, 2001) and, together with Hans Vlieghe and Cyriel Stroo, of Vlaamse meesters. Zes eeuwen schilderkunst (Leuven: Davidsfonds, 2004), she is currently completing Laocoön Reversed. Changing Beliefs on Temporality and the Experience of Time in New York Art of the 1960s, forthcoming in 2005 from Leuven University Press. Her photographic research is focussed on photography's contribution to the confusion of the artistic genres in postwar art and on the medium's critical function in contemporary art. She regularly publishes on this topic, among others in L&B, Obscuur, A-Prior and I[&]N. She is a member of the purchasing committee at the Antwerp Photomuseum and a contributing editor to Fotomuseum Magazine.

Alice Evermore (°USA) moved from New York City to Brussels in 1996. She has since published four book projects and participated in numerous collaborations with artists, musicians and performers.
The poetry of Alice Evermore draws upon references that range from individual duality to modern physics. By blending together scientific terminology with innate self-questioning, she puts together a bizarre infusion of primal wonder and contemporary understanding.
In the piece, VISITATION, a narrator explores a series of vacated places where "inescapable things have happened". Ultimately, external wonder becomes self-reflexive, as she ponders the nature of her own unavoidable appointment with fate.

© 2004 by Leuven University Press / Presses Universitaires de Louvain /
Universitaire Pers Leuven
Blijde-Inkomststraat 5, B-3000 Leuven (Belgium)

ISBN 90 5867437 1
D/2004/1869/87
NUR: 652, 651, 646, 649, 653

Lay-out: Stefan Siffer

Lieven Gevaert Research Centre
Arts Faculty K.U.Leuven
Blijde Inkomststraat 21
B-3000 Leuven
tel: 32 (0)16 32 48 79
fax: 32 (0) 16 3 2 48 72

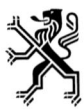
Published with the support of the Flemish Community